STATUS AND EMPOWERMENT OF THE GIRL CHILD

ASPECTS IN CROSS-CULTURAL CONTEXT

STATUS AND EMPOWERMENT OF THE GIRL CHILD

ASPECTS IN CROSS-CULTURAL CONTEXT

By

N.K. Behura

R.P. Mohanty

Nabakrushna Choudhury Centre for Development Studies, Orissa Bhubaneswar–751 013

DISCOVERY PUBLISHING HOUSE

NEW DELHI-110002

First Published-2005

ISBN 81-7141-961-5

Published by

DISCOVERY PUBLISHING HOUSE
4831/24, Ansari Road, Prahlad Street,
Darya Ganj, New Delhi-110002 (India)
Phone: 23279245 • Fax: 91-11-23253475
E-mail:dphtemp@indiatimes.com

Printed at:

Amit Enterprises, Delhi

Foreword

Over the years, particularly during the last hundred and fifty years, Indologists, Sociologists, Anthropologists, Historiographers have turned their attention to assess the problems plaguing women in the traditional Indian society. When some writers have highlighted the prevalent inequality, discrimination and exploitation suffered by women owing to the orthodox attitudes of male and the existing customs, conventions and traditions etc., others have attempted to examine women's status in the light of their new legal rights in the Hindu society. Rigidity of customs and social practices is so strong that changes till now are insignificant. Therefore, howsoever, high the status of women might have been raised under the law, in actual practice, women in large number of cases continue to suffer from discriminations which restrict their talent and ability to contribute to their respective families and societies. Gender inequality precludes growth of a healthy and prosperous society.

If gender inequality in Indian societies persists, it will retard all progress. There, it has to be eliminated not only by enacting laws but also by creating awareness and consciousness among the masses.

The present study has attempted to assess the ground situation of women as regards their legal rights and extent to which they actually enjoy the social, economic and political rights. The study has been conducted in five fringe villages and two slums of Bhubaneswar city covering 200 households of upper castes group, middle order castes group and some SC and ST households. The result of the study shows that the girl child and women are still deprived of, by their male counterparts even after more than 55 years of independence of the country. However, I hope the findings of this report will be very useful to the academicians, researchers, development administrators and to all those who are actively engaged and interested in the development of women. It is a micro-study with macro-implications.

I take great pleasure in thanking Prof. N.K. Behura, Honorary Fellow of NKC Centre for Development Studies Orissa, and Dr. R.P. Mohanty of the centre for the immense trouble they have taken in preparing the study against immense odds. Even though Prof. Behura is an Honorary Fellow, he takes considerable interest in promoting research scholars. I am also happy that Dr. R.P. Mohanty has been taking keen interest in research activity of the Centre. Both of them deserve our commendation.

(Prof. B. Misra)
Former Director and Chairman
and at present Research Advisor,
N.K.C. Centre for Development Studies, Orissa

Preface

Sex is a biological factor, which is concerned with reproduction and perpetuation of human-kind. Gender is a social and cultural construct grown over millions of years. Gender roles in societies are inculcated through socializations and enculturation processes. If the objectives and contents of socialization and enculturation currently in vogue are not changed, the current mode of gender inequality will persist. Gender discrimination is pernicious, and therefore, it has to go. Gender equality can be achieved through empowerment of women, specially by educating them and making them joint owners of property along with men. And further, they be fully involved in all the domestic decision-making processes. Gender inequality stems from the social structural elements. Descent is counted in the male line in patrilineal societies where property is inherited and passed in the male line. Authority is bequeathed to male descendants on the basis of primogeniture rule. Thus, the concept of discrimination implies that the problem is part of the socio-cultural system, which is acceptable to all. Discrimination is aglore for male chauvinism and physical prowess. People render only lip-service to the fact of women's emancipation, but practise discrimination with alacrity. No society will progress and develop in a balanced manner if discrimination against girl children and women continues. The present study has been undertaken to find out the degree and nature of discrimination against girl children and women in the fringe villages of the capital city of Bhubaneswar, which is supposed to be an enlightened area.

Discrimination against girl children and women in Indian society is an integral part of Indian mind-set that garners rational male dominance. And what is galling is that even after 57 years of

Indian independence the rate of female literacy is abysmally low and rise of atrocities on women continues. No society will develop if nearly half of its population is disadvantaged. According to the State of World Population Report, 1991, women can be empowered by enabling them to exercise certain choices: choices about if and when to get married; choices about education; creation of employment opportunities for them; right to control social and physical environment; choices abut if and when to get pregnant and family size. True empowerment can be ensured if men in different social statuses help to promote a healthy social environment based on gender equality, which is free from coercion, violence and abuse.

Fringe villages have burden exposure and exhibit relatively better literacy rates than interior villages. Men is the fringe villages are expected to be progressive. The present study is an explorative one, which aims to find out the nature of discrimination against girl children and women in such villages.

Thus, it was propitious for us to undertake such a crucial study. But we could not touch some of the important and noteworthy aspects of the study since it was an internal project based on very limited funds and manpower. Moreover, it was a time-bound project supposed to have been completed only within few months.

We sincerely express our deep and profound gratitude to Prof. B. Misra, the former Chairman, Nabakrushna Choudhury Centre for Development Studies, and Prof. G.C. Kar, the former Director of the institute for co-operating us to undertake the study.

We are extremely grateful to our informants who have helped us in many ways to collect data smoothly during the fieldwork. We are also very grateful to Shri Baikuntha Nath Sal and Shri Samir Kumar Digal who have helped us in data collection on request.

We hope that this piece of work, which is the second in the 'Social Problems Series', will be useful to the researchers, academicians, development administrators, NGO activities, social workers and also to all those who are interested in gender studies and are engaged in removing the discrimination prevailing against the girl child and woman in Indian society.

N.K. Behura

R.P. Mohanty

Contents

1

Introduction

Gender inequality is a ubiquitous global phenomenon everywhere. In every sphere of life women exist as subservient to men and thus, the men enjoy a superior social status as compared to their women counterparts. Persistence of this disparity between men and women is not because of any single reason rather there are various social and bio-cultural reasons responsible for this. Ahuja points out that the low social status of women in India is an offshoot of the result of illiteracy, economic dependency, caste restrictions, religious prohibitions, lack of leadership quality and apathetic and callous attitude of males (1992: 2). But Ghose is of the opinion that myths, legends, and social laws of Hinduism have given the Indian women a lower position in the society (1994: 3). However, Everett (1981), as referred by Ahuja (1992: 2), identifies five specific reasons for this. These are: Hindu religion, caste system, joint family system, Islamic rules, and British colonialism. But to our mind, some other phenomena strike as the basic and core factors for which male and female do not enjoy equal rights and, therefore, they are bestowed with differential social status even though they are considered as two sides of the same coin in human civilization. These factors may be discussed under the following broad headings:

(i) The functional nature of society and the women;

(ii) Physiological and biological composition of human body and the women;

(iii) The role of ancient law-makers, caste based culture and the women; and

(iv) The notion of remaining loyal and truthful to husband, like a *sati*, following the path of any of the five ancient Indian *Sati*-women, viz, Ahalya, Draupadi, Tara, Kunti and Mandodari, who are traditionally considered as the model of perfection of womanhood for the well-being of their respective husbands.

Most of the Indian societies are primarily patriarchal, patrilineal, and patrilocal, and therefore such societies are also patronymic in nature. These peculiarities signify concentration of power and authority system on males, inheritance of property and higher social status in the male-line, and the custom of residing of the female spouse at the home of her husband after marriage. So, women are to obey and pay sufficient respect to their husbands or male heads in their in-law's house; they are to ritually fast during the ancestral worship of the dead falling in the lineage of their respective husbands, even though they have not seen any of them during their lifetime and know them personally, and they are to stay permanently in the house of their husbands after marriage. If, for any reason, like a dispute with husband because of his immoral nature and infidelity or for any other reason, a married woman desires to comeback and stay with her parents, her parents do not permit this since society looks down upon such a woman even though she is innocent and very moral. She is motivated to go back and adjust herself with her husband or she is motivated to make all efforts to bring her husband to right path. Thus, this is the way how a woman has to sacrifice her life and accommodate herself against all odds of life for the sake of her husband. Hence, in these societies women exist only as instruments and obsequious to men and as such they are treated by the society as persons to provide pleasure and social support to the men by the way of their subservience.

A woman is considered as a lesser or weaker sex. The biological composition of her body and physical get-up is specific since the muscular part of her body is made up of softer tissues and her physical get-up designed to bear children and for upbringing them. For this, she remains unable to fight with a man, and as such, she does not think of struggling physically with her male counterparts for survival. Knowing her physical limitations, she surrenders herself before a male and foresees her future with her husband; a stronger sex. However, being a person of weaker sex, her roles, duties and responsibilities remain confined to the indoor-world, i.e. looking after children and undertaking the domestic chores. And she has to work under her husband. By the way, she is often ill-treated, abused and even in many cases not considered as a human being at par with her husband or a man. Her sorrows and sufferings remain throughout her lifetime, i.e. from birth to death.

If we consider the women being weaker sex as a natural phenomenon, it seems to be difficult to believe the contemporary sociologists who have established the theory of prevalence of high social status of women in matriarchal, matrilineal and matrilocal societies. Of course, it may be very true that in such societies, socially the women might be enjoying a superior status than their male counterparts because of the provision of social and economic security they enjoy by their tradition, but certainly because of their being the weaker sex, in many such societies (viz Khasi, Garo, Jayantia, Namboodiris, Nairs, Ezhevas etc.) where female-headship or authority is recognised, inheritance of property comes in the female-line and the male spouse has to leave his parent's home and reside permanently with his wife at his in-law's home, they are also ill-treated, abused and physically tortured by the males. This happens mainly because the natural strength and the muscle power of men are more than those of the women, and this superiority cannot be simply suppressed by mere exercise of unnatural or man-made social rule and regulations.

From the above discussion, it is now understood that the nature of the society on one hand and the biological and physical get-up of human body on the other, have been in many ways responsible for creation of gender inequality in traditional societies. However, apart from these two aspects, another factor is there which is equally important in Indian context, i.e. the godlike role of ancient Hindu law-makers, namely Yagvalkya and Manu who have prescribed a series of code of conduct for the women in various religious scriptures, which have, in course of time, become the cultural practice of various forms and thereby women have been inheriting a subordinate status since such scriptures came into existence either in written or unwritten form. Even to-day, most of the women of contemporary societies are traditionbound and do not like to violet the tradition set by such law-makers.

The laws and the tradition, which are set out for the women in *Manu-Smriti* seem to be very dishonourific and derogatory for them. Ghose has summarized the whole thrust of the philosophy expressed in this text. He says that, "the philosophy expressed in the *Manu-Smriti* can be linked to the symbolism of seed and earth. Man provides the seed, the essence, for the creation of the offspring. This seed determines the child's identity. The role of woman, like the earth, is simply to receive the seed and help it to grow. This implied that man is the lord, master, and provider. A woman is seen as nothing more than a commodity or a possession", (1991: 15). Further he has quoted the following stanza from the *Manu Smriti* to substantiate his conclusion.

"A woman must constantly worship her husband as a god, even though he is destitute of virtue of womanizer. A woman should be kept in dependency by her husband because by nature women are passionate and disloyal. Ideal woman are those who do not strive to break these bonds of control. The salvation and happiness of women revolve around their virtue and chastity as daughters, wives, and widows", (ibid).

The specifications made above signify how and what a woman should do and how the salvation and happiness of women depend on their nature, i.e. their loyalty towards their husbands. But this does not specify any specification regarding the conduct of men which they must maintain to have a better social life. This, otherwise means the supermacy of men over the women as they can do anything and hence, their happiness or salvation does not depend on their purity of character or personality or their husbandly devotion towards their wives.

Once a woman loses her chastity, she fails to keep up her prestige and the society looks down upon her. A disloyal woman is severely punished by her husband and even by the society or caste councils. Punishment to such women is also sanctioned by the caste *panchayats* even in contemporary societies. This is evident in many traditional and simple societies. Very recently a woman in South 24-Parganas was tonsured and her clothes were torn and thrown out for alleged adultery. This was done after the judgement of the local caste *panchayat* that sat in the village on 30th June, 1999. This news was published in the *Times of India*' on 28th July, '99. The paper points out that, "In an incident reminiscent of the dark middle ages, a *panchayat* in the Baruipur area of South 24-Parganas on June 30 decreed that a woman's hair be cropped off and she be thrown out of the locality for allegedly having an extramarital affair. But the suspected adulterer was let off without any punishment.

The incident happened at Chakarberia village. The woman was hauled up in front of the entire locality, her hair was chopped off and parts of her scalp were tonsured. She was then beaten up, her clothes were torn and thrown out.

Taslima Bibi, a housewife and mother of two, was accused of having an illicit affair with 23-year-old Rafique, a local youth. Her husband, Rahimtulla, a carpenter, worked elsewhere and came home once a week.

On June 29, Taslima was allegedly seen coming out of a house in the area with Rafique. Some villagers lodged a complaint with the *panchayat*. The next day she was brought in front of the *panchayat* and humiliated..." (*Times of India*, 28.7.99).

Surprisingly, even when the husband dies for any reason, the wife is immediately blamed and branded as an evil force as tradition considers the long life of husbands on the truthfulness and maintenance of chastity of wives. Tradition reveals the fact that if a woman is dutiful, truthful and loyal to her husband, like a *Sati*, she can bring longlife for her husband and prosperity for her family and such a woman can do anything which an untruthful or disloyal woman cannot do. In this context tradition has many instances to show how miracles can be achieved by the chasteful women and hence the necessity of remaining loyal and chasteful. Here, one of such instances may be referred to 'Eekhbaku was the eldest son of Manu, who, in course of time inherited the throne of the dynasty of his father. Sudeba, his wife was the most beautiful and a *patibrata* woman of the then time. She had earned a lot of *punya* by being very loyal and wifely devotional to her husband. One day, Eekhbaku went on a hunting expedition with his wife and a troop of soldiers. On the way, they came across of a huge wild boar that was roaming with its consort and about hundred offsprings. The soldiers attacked the boar and its family. But the boar killed a number of soldiers and injured many of them. It incited the king Eekhbaku to fight with it. The boar was killed by a heavy blow with his *gada* (mace). But a godly man came out of its dead body and vanished in the heaven. Now, the sow became very aggressive and fought with the king. But the king abstained himself from fighting with the sow since it was beyond his dignity to kill any she-creature. The soldiers fought with it and the sow bravely faced them but lastly it fell down. The queen Sudeba was astonished to see the courage of it and went to pour some water in the mouth of the animal. But surprisingly the sow told like a human being "this is the result of my past life. I was a beautiful daughter of a Brahman; Basudeva. I married a man. But my beauty attracted a number of men. It demoralized me and I enjoyed life with them. On knowing about my disloyalty, my husband left me and married another woman. In course of time, I became old and lost my beauty. Thereafter nobody bothered me. Suddenly, one day I met my husband. He narrated all the story to his second wife. His second wife was very loyal to him. She loved me so much that I could not bear upon that and I collapsed. Then I got this sinful sow life... Now, if you can kindly donate me the *punya* of at least one year you have earned as a chasteful wife, I would get salvation from this sinful life. Queen Sudeba did so with the permission of her husband. The sow became a woman and went to the heaven in a 'divinely chariot' (The Samaj, 1999: 1). This instance shows how perfect wifely service of women can make impossible matters possible that is highly essential for the benefit of self, husband and other family members. However, in the present era, this type of instance does not happen. Still then the people believe in the past tradition that has shaped up the present one. And now, every man looks for such an ideal wife who should be very truthful and loyal. But men have the liberty to go to any woman still then they demand chasteful character of their wives. Of course, this ideology seems to be very illogical. Hence, very often it creates a psychological clash between spouses but ultimately the wife has to surrender. This fact seems to be true, because of their economic dependence on men, and also because of their being the weaker sex, their inability to fight with men and lead life independently without the physical support of men, the stronger sex. If somehow the wife becomes frustrated and neglects her duty because of her husband's nature, she is uncared for, abused, tortured or she can be divorced and in that case she is looked down by the society.

Human societies are dominated by man. Tradition expects that the wife of a person must die before her husband and as such each and every married women like that their husbands must outlive them. If the husband dies first, it was the duty of the widow to sacrifice herself in the pyre of her dead husband as *sati*.

In the past it was not simply expected from the women that they must remain chasteful to their husbands rather the wives had to voluntarily sacrifice themselves on the pyre of their dead husbands since they did not have the right to remarry or even think of any man as a part of their eternal love. If any of them was not passing through this rite of *Sati*, society was compelling them to do so. This tradition even marched from the remote past to the present day. It is very recently that such an event occurred in 1987 when Roop Kunwar (18) of a village, namely Deovala in Rajsthan was dragged to commit *Sati*, i.e. sacrifice of self on the pyre of her dead husband (cf. Ghose, 1991: 71).

However, at present the practice of *Sati* is very rare. But, even though the widow lives after the death of her husband, her social status becomes very low as compared to other women. As a widow, she has to behave in a particular order following the rigid code of conducts of the society so that nothing negative happens to the family members or to any of the villagers.

Even now, there are many societies in India, particularly in Rajasthan where child marriages are rampant and the life of girl children are simply neglected and spoiled for the sake of pleasure in male-dominated societies. Here, a child widow is branded as a *prostitute* even though she is physically immature to have sex or is not aware of sex (ibid: 121). These facts reveal how heinously the society has graded the women and look upon them for absolute ownership and use them like commodities by the men.

A woman who is unable to give birth to a male child to the householder or her husband, is considered as an inauspicious or evil force. In such a case she is tortured and her status in the family is reduced to a very low position. This is rampant in almost all the Indian societies. In a news item published in the *The Samaj* on 21st July, 1991 (a vernacular newspaper, published from Cuttack), signifies that a woman who has given birth to five daughters, is severely tortured by her husband even after 16 years of her marriage. She is threatened to be divorced since her husband has looked at another lady who can presumably give her a male child. However, presently there are many societies, where ritually a girl child is considered as *Laxmi*, but surprisingly when a girl baby is born, her suffering starts soon after she touches the ground on her birth. She does not provide much pleasure to her parents or to the other kins. And as such her birth is not celebrated with joy and pomp, rather in many cases, her arrival is considered as a mundane affair. She is considered as an economic and physical burden in Hindu societies as she leaves her natal home after her marriage, and therefore, girl-infanticide has been in existence in India since very long time. Puri's work signifies that girl infants in various parts of our country are known to have been killed by being deprived of major nourishment or even by rubbing poison on the mother's breasts Ghose (1998: 7) is of the same opinion. He cites a thrilling fact on female infanticide in Rajasthan. He has noted that there is a mound called 'Gudiyon Ka Tilla' or the mound of dolls, near certain hamlets in the said state. This is the place where unwanted female babies are buried (1994: 105).

Today, government has banned infanticide of any sex. Even it has also put strict restriction on sex-determination tests at the foetal stage. Still then sex-determination at this stage is done and girl foeticide is on the rise both among the poor as well as affluent societies throughout the country because of various factors, like the burden of dowry on the marriage of girl being the most important one (cf. Uni, 1998: 7). Those who are not able to kill their girl children either because of their kind-heartedness or because of their ignorance on the process of foeticide or infanticide, keep their girl children but discriminate them on various spheres of life. As socially as well as, economically she is not equated with a male child and is preferred to make her carried on domestic chores, she is not provided with education, not even basic or minimum education, while at the same time much care is taken and sincere efforts are made for the higher education of her brother. This happens mainly because a girl child leaves her natal home and goes to her husband's home after her marriage and as a result, parents do not like to spend much money on her education rather train her how to manage home as a housewife. However, she is not only deprived of education but also her nutritional status is also palpably low since the parental or societal attitude towards her food intake is very discriminatory and distressing. As an infant she is breast fed for a shorter period and a lion's share of mother's milk is reserved for her elder or younger brother who are equally or even less dependent on that for survival. On the attainment of childhood, the notion of 'inferiority complex' as compared to a boy child is injected into her mind by the way of discriminatory process of socialization and even imparting of various negative cultural values or enforcing physical deprivation of certain opportunities. As for example, most often she is underfed or given less food than what her brother is provided with. Even she is not permitted to take food before her brother comes from the school or the playground and is fed properly. No matter, what happens to her even if she is overworked, fatigued, and feels hungry. She has to wait for her brother and she may take the remnants in the same dish since the remnants of her brother cannot be disposed off otherwise. This cultural deprivation never leaves her until her death. Even when she marries and leaves her parent's home, she carries the same social value with her and acts accordingly at her in-law's home. But here, she remains deprived for another man; her husband, in the same way she was being treated at her parent's house for the well-being of her brothers. Here, she becomes a wife, a daughter-in-law, an aunt, a mother and so on and so forth. As such her social and cultural role, duty and responsibilities are multiplied and likewise, the probability of being deprived of or discriminated is increased. As a wife, daughter-in-law, or even as in different social bodies to different kins, she has to perform in a particular order that the society approves. Otherwise she is considered as an evil being. She has to cook and serve food to all the members. But surprisingly she has to take her own food after all of them are 'properly and satisfactorily' fed. She cannot reserve a share of any food for herself before they are fed, rather, she has to adjust with what is left at the end. If nothing is left, she can take some other food if she likes, but certainly not superior food than what she has served to other family members. If she can do like this, she is respected and regarded by all her family members, otherwise she is not considered as an ideal person—a wife, a daughter-in-law, an aunt etc. And in that case she may be ill treated.

Apart from the above code of conduct, she is expected to undergo various rites and practices, rituals and feasts for the well-being of her family members, particularly her husband. On the contrary there is no such rite or feasting socially sanctioned for a husband which he must perform for the welfare of his wife as a token of reciprocity. This otherwise reveals the fact as to how a woman is socially exploited for satisfying the male-oriented ego of the society where the ego is predetermined by the tradition.

At the public fronts, the social status of a woman is also equally discriminatory and even derogatory. This is evident in many forms, both within and outside their own society. As for example, they are not permitted to hold and attend any public meeting and undertake any work thereupon without the permission of their male counterparts. Traditionally they are excluded from the members of the village *panchayats* and even not permitted to perform any ritual for the caste tutelary deities at the village or community levels since the ritual service for such deities are confined to the male folks only. What is more astonishing is that in a particular sect of Islamic religion, the women are not permitted to see the outer world since a rigorous social system, like *purdah* is prevalent among them. This system compels them to use a screen in front of their face whenever they are out of their home. Once they violate the norm, the result becomes very serious. These, strictures are, however, culture and religion based, but their lower status, irrespective of culture or religion, is clearly visible when in many traditional poor tribal caste and peasant societies, their labour is not equated with those of the men. Surprisingly they are paid much less wage for the same or similar work done by their male co-workers. This situation is more serious in urban informal sectors and urban fringes where the local brokers and labour contractors play an important role. The tribal women who are less intelligent, economically weak and less clever than others fall pray to these agents. Their labour is extracted to the highest possible extent but they are not paid equal wage with men, and often, the actual wage fixed by the government; many times paid less wage than what they sign by their thumb impression, not paid wages in time even if an informal contract is made for payment of wages weekly or daily or before formal initiation of the work.

In order to eradicate these social discrepancies from the society, Government of India has provided various legislative measures by which the women can be empowered and hence can come out into the mainstream at par with the men. Some of the important legislations enacted after independence of India for the welfare of women and for equalizing them with men are— Factories Act, 1948; Plantation Labour Act, 1951; Mines Act, 1952; Hindu Marriage Act, 1955; Hindu Succession Act, 1956; Child Marriage Restraint Act, 1976; Equal Remuneration Act, 1976; Dowry Prohibition Act, 1961; *Sati* Prevention Act, 1987; etc. Apart from all these legislations, government has also made various provisions, like basic education for all by 2000 A.D., reduction of malnutrition level, adult literacy for both the sexes, empowerment of the females to prevent unwanted pregnancies, special health and nutritional programmes for females during various stages of their life, viz early childhood, adolescence, pregnancy and lactation, feeling of essential knowledge and life skills for all families etc. But instead of implementation of all these measures, not much have yet been achieved.

Most of the girl children in several societies are still deprived of education and hence their future is confined to the dark cage of domestic fore. Still then one cannot generalize the status of Indian women since in this country we have various social segments and a strong base of caste hierarchy, depending on which the status of women is based upon. So, it is now important to see actually to what extent the girl children and the women of different social segments, like upper caste Hindu communities, caste Hindu peasants, ex-untouchable communities and the Scheduled Tribe Communities, have come forward through the provisions of government avenues and how do they look at the modern world.

Aims and Objective of the Study

The broad aims and objectives of the present study are six-fold. These are, to find out:

(a) to notion of culturally determined mode of behaviour for male and female children, that is, gender equality and 'inequality',

(b) the educational deprivation of the girl child and the associated socio-cultural factors,

(c) the culture of diet and eating pattern relating to the girl child and a boy child,

(d) the level of discrimination on health sector in relation to preferential treatment process,

(e) the utilization of income and exploitation of labour,

(f) the levels of awareness of men and women on the protective measures and their views, and

(g) to formulate an action plan model for the well-being of the girl children and the women.

The Study Universe and Methodology

The Study Universe

The universe of the study constitutes a total number of 200 households: 50 each from upper caste Hindu Community (Brahman), caste Hindu peasant community (Chasa), Scheduled Caste community (Bauri) and Scheduled Tribe community (Santal).

Sampling Procedure

The study is confined to five multi-caste Hindu villages located on the outskirts of Bhubaneswar city, and two slums located within its municipal boundary. These are all situated in Bhubaneswar block of Khurdha district of the state of Orissa.

All the five multi-caste Hindu villages were selected on the purposive random sampling basis depending upon the constitution of caste institutions. Importance was given to select those villages that constituted upper caste Hindu households, caste Hindu peasant households and households belonging to Scheduled Caste communities. Because such villages are considered as ideal one since all the traditional peculiarities of Indian villages are visible in these bases. Since, traditionally the coastal villages do not constitute tribal population, and as a part of the objectives of the study to assess the social situation of the girl children and the women cross-culturally, we have purposively selected two slums where such population (tribal) are found.

As to the selection of households, emphasis was given on those households that had children of either sex and had adult women and men as wife and husband. This provision was made to enable us to visualize as to how the parents look at their male and female children and how do they look at each other as husband and wife.

Research Design and Use of Research Tools

The whole population of each community has been divided into two parts, viz children and adult. Then the child population is sub-divided into two parts—girl children and boy children. Similarly, the adult population has also been sub-divided into two parts—women and men. Thereafter, inter-and-intra community comparison has been made between girl and boy children and also between women and men of each community. Likewise, in order to focus the cross-cultural variations, comparison has also been made amongst the girls and also amongst the women of these four communities.

The present study has made use of a specific schedule for recording the socio-economic information of the study-population. Apart from this, some case studies have been recorded and group discussions were made. While collecting data, much importance was given to both the participatory as well as non-participatory observation methods, so as to understand the ways of deprivation and discrimination prevalent amongst the children, and also amongst the women of the said communities.

Nature of the Study

The nature of the present research work is of one-time cross-cultural, since it has intended to focus a comparative picture of the social status of the girl children and the women of different ethnic groups residing in similar social environments. At the same time, it is also a cross-sectional study, as it has intended to show the disparities existing between sexes within each of ethnic groups mentioned above.

Literature Survey

There are many studies available on various facets of women's problem. But the studies conducted on the status and empowerment of the girl children and women are few.

Sachchidananda and Sinha (1984) have made a study on the women to examine the level of their awareness on different constitutional provisions enacted for their well-being at different times. They have also attempted to show the sources of their awareness, attitudinal perspectives towards such provisions and the reaction of men on the provision made for empowering the women. The result of their study is based on the response of a total number of 960 women and 960 men drawn from four different cultural zones of the state of Bihar; viz Magahi (Gaya district), Bhojpur (Bhojpur districts), Maithili (Madhubani district) and Tribal (Ranchi district).

The conclusion arrived in the study reveals some amazing features. Even after lapse of many decades of independence of India, most of the women have still remained ignorant of their legal rights. Likewise, the men also do not know much about the legislations provided for the upliftment of women. This has caused the women to still remain as subservient to men. Surprisingly, while many laws were favoured by the women, some were rejected and looked down upon by them because of their self-submission to the traditional way of life; this is because of lack of education and awareness. On the contrary, most of the men reacted sharply towards the social legislations made for the women since they did not like to equalize the women with them.

Karlekar (1987) has made a study on the sweeper women, residing in Delhi, who subsist on their traditional occupation. He has taken a total number of 80 samples and attempts to show the impact of independence on the living conditions of these women, difficulties involved in their employment and working conditions. Finally, he also suggests an action plan for their all-round development.

He concludes that employment is indispensable for the poor women, like sweepers who contribute substantially a large amount to their family's income. And for this, they are to toil for longer hours than the men. And they even undertake many difficult works for the sake of their family members. But still then they are not honoured much by their husbands, and in many cases, they are not consulted in major decisions of the family. Thus, they lead a pitiable and miserable life.

Arputhamurthy (1990) makes a study to examine the women agricultural labourers pertaining to paddy cultivation in Madurai district of Tamil Nadu, who were discriminated on the basis of sex. She has integrated the theoretical base in her analysis on the field-based data. Her objectives were four-fold, viz: (i) to find out the different types of agricultural operations carried out by the men and women, (ii) to find out the social prejudices traditionally attached in allotting less paid agricultural operations to women and more paid operations to men through sexual division of labour, (iii) to find out the extent of wage differential existing between men and women doing various agricultural operations and justification of such differences, and (iv) to examine whether wage differential exists because of difference in the levels of agricultural development and job segregation by sex in the study area.

She concludes that in rural sectors, division of labour leads to job segregation that creates disparity in wage rates between sexes. Normally jobs associated with high prestige and high wage are assigned to the men and the women are given jobs involved with less prestige and hence less wage. These factors have significantly lowered the social status of women in traditional societies.

In opposition to the above study on rural women, Sood (1991) has undertaken a study in urban sectors. She has studied four category of employed women, viz higher (teachers in the university), higher middle (Research assistants, library assistants, technical assistants, section officers etc.) middle (stenographers, typists etc.), and low-income persons (sweeper, peons etc.), confined to Jawaharlal Nehru University (JNU) campus, in order to understand the extent to which education and employment help in raising the status of women, relationship of women with their men counterparts, the nature and patterns of dominance existing among women particularly emanating from their economic and educational background, pattern of adjustment and the changes occurred in women's attitude.

She concludes that education on one hand and employment on the other, have together quenched women's quest for equality with men. But surprisingly educated and employed women themselves surrender to men supremacy because of their biological and physiological strength.

Bhadra (1992) has conducted a work on women tea plantation workers belonging to tribe and Nepali communities. She has analytically presented the factors responsible for entering of such women workers into the labour market and how their employment affect their daily social life.

She has discussed the problem and the trend of women labour participation in rural and urban occupational structures, both in organised and unorganised sectors and analyses various social components and dimensions of life, like, family, marriage, divorce and remarriage, family planning process, decision-making in the family, husband's attitude towards wife's employment, sharing of household responsibilities, economic contribution to family income, child care, socialization of children etc. She concludes that these women are dual workers, i.e. they are plantation workers and at the same time they are also housewives. And for this, their role in relation to the above components in management of daily life is very important and crucial. Still then they inherit a low social status and their dominance is not at all accepted by the men.

Gothoskar (1992) has edited a volume containing papers on struggles of women in the employment and in wage work. The volume contains a total number of 13 papers written by different workers. The paper of Vijan (1992) in this volume shows that the fish-workers struggle collectively for changing the role of women in such sectors. Priya (1992) points out that the situation of the women contract workers in Ennore Thermal Power Station is very crucial. Hence, the need for struggle for equal rights for such women is very essential.

Ahuja (1992) has made a study in 8 rural villages of Jaipur district, Rajsthan. His study covered a total sample of 753 women and 753 men.

The main purpose of his work was to explore the existing reality and develop hypotheses pertaining to awareness of social and constitutional rights on economic, social and political sectors of women, and satisfaction with the actual status they have in their respective societies. He concludes that even though the constitution has provided various protectional measures, most of the women and also men are not aware of those measures of the government. This has necessitated the social status of rural women almost unchanged.

Ghose's (1994) study is very informative on identifying the social situation of women in India. He has tried to visualise the status of Indian women of the present era through ancient and medieval periods and concludes that myths, culture etc. have been very influential in Indian society to give a lower social status to the women of this country.

Pant's (1995) study on the status of the girl children and the women of Uttar Pradesh shows some peculiarities. In his study, he has vividly described the demographic structure of these people with reference to the secondary data. He has also based his work with the primary information. He is of the opinion that health, nutrition and education are three important aspects which have invariably been adverse to the women and the factors responsible for these are mainly poverty and social conditions. These results in prejudices and negative attitudes towards women. So, he has laid much stress on the role of voluntary organisations and on the role of the government to improve the social condition of these persons and to take necessary steps to equalize them with men.

In a study, Purushothaman (1998) has synthesized the analytical part of his work with the existing social movement theory, development theory and the theories of the State. He has taken a case study of an informal network of a local NGO in Maharashtra and has analyzed the implications of the form and nature of such organisations for changing the power relations and fostering autonomy of women folk vis-a-vis men.

He concludes that centralization of power or centralized organisational forms as the base of contemporary social movement theory cannot bring about any change rather he emphasizes on decentralisation of power and informal organisational forms by which the participation of poor rural women in development process can be ensured and it would enable them to bargain for resources. Consequently, it would demand for a change in the state policy while at the same time it would protect the autonomy of women of rural societies.

Significance, Scope and Limitations of the Study

Women, as subservient to men have existed in our societies since remote past. Their low social position as compared to their male counterparts, as a challenging discipline has attracted many social scientists in India and abroad to work on this sector. At the present time, many have also advocated to make 'women studies' a separate discipline of study within the wider scope of anthropological and sociological perspectives. In many parts of the world, separate institutions have also been established with a view to understanding the problems of the women more specifically and pinpointedly. In Orissa, such an attempt has also been made and an institution has been dedicated for carrying out studies on the problem. Some scholars are also there in the state who are conducting studies on women from sociological view points. But certainly, anthropological studies on this area of the problem in Orissa are very rare. As a whole, the studies conducted on women either by the sociologists or by social anthropologists do not contribute much to establish any women based cross-cultural study that would throw some light on the status and empowerment of girl children and the women of contemporary societies, who, for centuries, have been neglected by the society and have remained unresearched from anthropological perspectives. For these basic reasons, the study seems to be very significant. But the scope of the study is not so broad since it constitutes a small sample size. However, the study would be very useful as a handbook to the academicians, researchers, action planners, administrators, NGOs activities and all those who are interested on the problems of the girl children and the women. This study will provide theoretical clues to future studies.

2

Profile of the Study Villages

Location of Study Villages

The study villages of the present piece of research work include five multi-caste Hindu villages, namely Raghunathpur, Kalarahanga, Daruthenga, Barimund and Khairapada and two slums, namely, Patharabandha and Salia Sahi of Bhubaneswar city. All these villages and slums are located in the Bhubaneswar block of Khurdha district. But when all the study villages are situated on the outskirts of Bhubaneswar city, i.e. outside the municipal boundary, both the slums are located within the municipal boundary.

From amongst the study villages, Khairapada and Barimund are located on the north-east corner, Daruthenga on the north-west corner and the rest two villages, viz Kalarahanga and Raghunathpur on the north side of the city. These villages fall within an approximate radius of 2-8 kilometers away from the municipal boundary of this city.

Basic Amenities and Infrastructure

Since all the study villages are located on the outskirts of Bhubaneswar city, the state capital of Orissa, these are all well connected with either *pucca* or *kutcha* roads. Hence, each village is jeepable and the people of these villages have greater access to Bhubaneswar as well as Cuttack cities.

Availability of educational facilities are important factors in the process of development. As a result, where there is lack of such facilities, there has been less development. But since all the study villages are located near the state capital of Orissa, the people of these villages have been enjoying better educational facilities, viz primary and high school education as well as college education since long. In each of the study villages, there is a primary school. High school education is also available in each village. There are some nearby colleges in which the people of the study villages are educating their children. The year of establishment of schools, colleges etc. and their distance from the study villages, are mentioned in Appendix 2, that may be referred to.

So far as the medical facility is concerned, the people of these villages normally depend on the local public health centres for treatment of minor diseases, but for the major ones, they depend on the capital hospital located at Unit-6 of Bhubaneswar city. However, many people of the villages, like Khairapada and Barimund depend on the hospitals and private clinics located in Cuttack city, since these villages are situated at an equi-distance from Bhubaneswar and Cuttack cities.

The two slums, viz Patharabandha and Salia Sahi are located inside the city in prime locations. Hence, the communication facility to these slums is very good but the communication facility available inside these slums is not so. However, since these slums are situated inside the city at prime locations, the residents of these slums have greater access to different places as compared to the people of the study villages.

There is no permanent educational institution run by government in any of these slums. But some remedial nursery and pre-nursery schools are in operation in these slums. These are primarily run by the local NGOs for last few years. However, since these slums are located within the city area, the people of these slums have better opportunities for educating their children in various educational institutions located around their habitations. But, they cannot avail these opportunities because of various limiting factors, the main being their poor economic condition. Similarly, there is no permanent medical institution inside their habitations. Still then, they have better scope of availing medical facilities from the local hospitals and public health centres or from the private clinics.

Households and Population Size

The data relating to total number of households and population size of study villages, as available from census of India office, Bhubaneswar, are presented in Table 2.1. It shows that out of all the study villages, the village Daruthenga consists of highest number of households, i.e. 551. It is followed by Raghunathpur, Kalarahanga, Barimund and Khairapada which consist of 151, 323, 312 and 79 households respectively. Since the village Daruthenga consists of highest number of households, it has maximum population, i.e. 2852. Similarly the village Khairapada bears minimum population compared to other villages as it constitutes lowest number of households. The population of other study villages in descending order come to be 2561 in Raghunathpur, 2091 in Barimund and 1985 in Kalarahanga. In all the villages, excepting the village of Daruthanga, the proportion of male population is more than the females.

So far as the case of slums is concerned, data (1997) available from Bhubaneswar Municipal Corporation (BMC) show that Patharabandha consists of as many as 1013 households and Salia Sahi has only 517 households. As a result the former slum has more population than the latter one that come to be 3831 and 1717 respectively.

Category of Population and Caste Composition

The most important aspect of the caste Hindu villages located in the coastal districts of Orissa is that in most of such villages, two broad social category of people live together. These are: (i) *Savarna* or general castes belonging to the *Varna* Organisation, i.e. Brahman (priest), Kshyatriya (ruling), Vaishya (trader) and Shudra (artisan and ritual service groups) and (ii) Scheduled Castes or *Avarna* or those who are outside the *Varna* organisation. In other districts, apart from these two broad social categories of people, another category of people, i.e Scheduled Tribes are found, who are migrants and are normally called as *Vanyaja, Vanyajati, Girijana* etc. So, since all the study villages are concentrated in a coastal district (Khurdha) of Orissa, the villages primarily comprise general castes belonging to the *Varna* organisation and Scheduled Castes who do not fall in this system. However, exceptionally there is one study village, like, Raghunathpur that includes some (26 or 5.8%) Scheduled Tribe households. These households have immigrated from other districts and settled down here with a hope of earning regular livelihood through wage-earning in Bhubaneswer or in the adjacent areas of the city.

Of the total five sample villages, there are 3 or 60 per cent villages, viz Raghunathpur, Barimund and Kalarahanga in which there are in between 20 to 28 per cent Scheduled Caste households. But in the rest two villages, viz Daruthenga and Khairapada, the proportion of Scheduled Castes households is more than 17 per cent but less than 20 per cent of the total households of the respective villages. The other households of each study village belong to the general castes (Table 2.2).

So far as the case of village-wise individual castes are concerned, each study village is multi-ethnic in nature. In the village Raghunathpur, there are 16 castes. Of these, 11 (68.75%) are general castes, 4 (25%) belong to Scheduled Caste communities, and the rest 1 (6.25%) belong to a Scheduled Tribe community. The village Kalarahanga has a total number of 15 castes belonging to different social strata of the caste hierarchy. But when it has as many as 11 (73.33%) general caste communities, the rest 4 (26.67%) are found to be Scheduled Caste communities. In the next village, i.e. Barimund, of the total 15 castes, 9 (60%) castes belong to general caste communities and the rest 6(10%) are Scheduled Caste communities. The village Daruthenga is found to constitute highest number of castes that comes to be as many as 18 in number. Of these, 13 (72.22%) are general castes and the rest 5 (27.78%) are Scheduled Caste communities.

Among the Scheduled Caste communities, the Bauris, who work as agricultural labourers, are found to be an important community in all the study villages excepting the village Raghunathpur, since, numerically they are found in highest number of households in those villages. In the village Raghunathpur, the Keuta (fisherman) people dominate other Scheduled Caste communities. So far as the numerical strength of individual castes in respect of their total number of households is concerned, it is found that amongst the general castes, the Chasa or agricultural caste (33.18%) in Raghunathpur, Gauda or milkman (28.81%) in Kalarahanga, Brahman or priest (25.56%) in Barimund and Khandayat or militia (23.31%) in Daruthenga dominate the village population (Table 2.3). But socially the *Brahmans* are found to be the most important caste in all the villages. However, since economy plays an important role in status identification and in *Jajmani* system prevalent in rural orissa, a different picture comes into the fore. In the village Raghunathpur and Daruthenga, the Khandayat people dominate the whole village since ownership of most of the landed properties remain with them. However, in the rest of the villages, viz Kalarahanga and Barimund, apart from occupying the super-most social status, economically the Brahmans of these villages are also found to be very sound and hence, they dominate other castes, both socially as well as economically.

The caste composition in the slums has been presented in Table 2.4. It is observed that there are as many as 26 caste communities of which 15 (57.19%) belong to the general castes, 8 (30.77%) belong to different Scheduled Caste communities and the rest 6 (23.68%) are various Scheduled Tribe communities. Apart from these 26 caste communities there are 5 categories of population who are unclassified. They are Bihari, Bengali, Muslim, Telegu and Nepali.

The major Scheduled Tribes residing in Patharabandha slum are: Kolha (198 households or 18.71%), Santal (81 or 7.19%), Munda (16 or 1.51%) and the major Scheduled Caste communities of this slum are: Hadi (105 or 9.92%), Keuta (14 or 1.32%), and Kandara (12 or 1.13%). Among the other or general castes, Chasa (106 or 10.2%), Khandayat (99 or 9.36%), Gauda (89 or 8.41%), Karana (35 or 3.31%), Badhei (32 or 3.02%), Brahman (28 or 2.65%), Kamara (14 or 1.32%), Teli (12 or 1.13%), Barika (11 or 1.04%) and Kansari (11 or 1.04%) are found to be important communities who have more than 1 per cent but less than 11 per cent households of the total 1058 households of the slum (Table: 2.4).

Table—2.1: Population profile of the study villages and slums

Sl. No.	*Village slum*	*Total households*	*Population*		
			Male	*Female*	*Total*
(1)	*(2)*	*(3)*	*(4)*	*(5)*	*(6)*
1.	Kalarahanga	323	1019 (51.31)	966 (48.66)	1985 (100.00)
2.	Raghunathpur	454	1306 (50.94)	1258 (49.06)	2564 (100.00)
3.	Khairapada	79	255 (50.80)	247 (49.20)	502 (100.00)
4.	Barimund	312	1057 (50.18)	1037 (49.52)	2094 (100.00)
5.	Daruthenga	551	1424 (49.93)	1428 (50.07)	2852 (100.00)
6.	Patharabandha (slum)	1013	NA	NA	3834 (100.00)
7.	Salia Sahi (slum)	517	NA	NA	1747 (100.00)

Note: Figures in brackets represent %age.

Source: *(i)* From Sl. No. 1-5, village census abstracts, Bhubaneswar block (unpublished) Census of India, Bhubaneswar.

(ii) From Sl. No. 6-7, Bhubaneswar Municipal Corporation, 1997.

Table—2.2: Study villages according to category of population

Sl. No.	Villages/slums	Category of population (in HHs)			Total
		SC	ST	OC	
(1)	(2)	(3)	(4)	(5)	(6)
1.	Kalarahanga	66 (20.69)	–	253 (79.31)	319 (100.00)
2.	Raghunathpur	121 (27.01)	26 (5.80)	301 (67.19)	448 (100.00)
3.	Khairapada				
4.	Barimund	58 (26.01)	–	165 (73.99)	223 (100.00)
5.	Daruthenga	79 (17.21)	–	380 (82.79)	459 (100.00)
6.	Patharabandha (slum)	183 (17.30)	297 (28.07)	578 (54.63)	1058 (100.00)
7.	Salia Sahi (slum)	–	–	–	517 (100.00)

Note: Figures in brackets represent %age.

Source: (i) From 1-5, local Panchayat office

(ii) Data in Sl. No. 6 from the Secretary Patharabandha slum, 1999.

(iii) Data in Sl. No. 7 from Bhubaneswar Municipal Corporation, 1997.

Table—2.3: Caste composition in study villages according to households

Sl. No.	Castes	Villages				
		Raghunathpur	*Kalarahanga*	*Barimund*	*Khairapada*	*Daruthenga*
(1)	(2)	(3)	(4)	(5)	(6)	(7)
A.	*OCs*					
1.	Badhei (Carpenter)	–	7 (2.19)	–		6 (1.31)
2.	Barika (Barber)	2 (0.45)	13 (4.08)	13 (5.83)		14 (3.05)
3.	Brahman (Priest)	23 (5.13)	51 (15.99)	57 (25.56)		20 (4.36)
4.	Chasa (Agriculturist)	150 (33.48)	33 (10.34)	40 (17.94)		101 (22.00)
5.	Gauda (Milkman)	7 (1.56)	92 (28.84)	12 (5.38)		9 (1.96)
6.	Gudia (Confectioner)	25 (5.58)	10 (3.13)	1 (0.45)		4 (0.87)
7.	Jyotish (Astrologer)	2 (0.45)	10 (3.13)	–		1 (0.22)
8.	Kamara (Blacksmith)	2 (0.45)	–	1 (0.45)		2 (0.44)
9.	Karana (Scribe)	4 (0.89)	1 (0.31)	–		32 (6.97)
10.	Khandayat (Militia)	83 (18.53)	8 (2.51)	10 (4.48)		107 (23.31)
11.	Mali (Flourist)	–	–	–		10 (2.18)
12.	Patra (Petty trader)	–	–	18 (8.07)		–
13.	Tanti (Weaver)	–	19 (5.96)	–		6 (1.31)
14.	Teli (Oil crusher)	3 (0.67)	9 (2.82)	8 (3.59)		67 (14.60)
	Sub-Total	301 (67.19)	253 (79.31)	165 (73.99)		380 (82.79)

(Contd...)

(1)	(2)	(3)	(4)	(5)	(6)	(7)
B.	*SCs*					
1.	Bauri (Agricultural labourer)	49 (10.94)	50 (15.67)	24 (10.76)		54 (11.76)
2.	Dhoba (Washerman)	4 (0.89)	4 (1.25)	4 (1.79)		5 (1.09)
3.	Dom (Hider)	–	–	13 (5.83)		–
4.	Hadi (Nightsoil) remover	2 (0.45)	2 (0.63)	–		2 (0.44)
5.	Kandara (Village watchman)	–	–	10 (4.48)		–
6.	Keuta (Fisherman)	66 (14.73)	10 (3.13)	7 (3.14)		18 (3.92)
	Sub-Total	121 (27.01)	66 (20.69)	58 (26.01)		79 (17.21)
C.	*STs*					
1.	Saor	26 (5.80)	–	–	–	–
	Total	*448 (100.00)*	*319 (100.00)*	*223 (100.00)*	*79 (100.00)*	*459 (100.00)*

Note: Figures in brackets represent % age.

Source: Local Panchayat Office.

Table—2.4: Caste composition in study slums (Patharabandha) according to households

Sl No.	*Castes*	*Toral households*	*% age*
(1)	(2)	(3)	(4)
A.	OCs		
1.	Badhei (Carpenter)	32	3.02
2.	Bania (Goldsmith)	5	0.42
3.	Barika (Barber)	11	1.04
4.	Brahman (Priest)	28	2.65
5.	Chasa (Agriculturist)	106	10.2
6.	Gauda (Milkman)	89	8.41
7.	Kachra (Bangle seller)	1	0.95
8.	Kamara (Blacksmith)	14	1.32
9.	Kansari (Brazier)	11	1.04
10.	Karana (Scribe)	35	3.31
11.	Khandayat (Militia)	99	9.36
12.	Mali (Flowrist)	6	0.57
13.	Patra (Petty trader)	1	0.95
14.	Tanti (Weaver)	6	0.57
15.	Teli (Oil crusher)	12	1.13
	Sub-Total	*456*	*43.10*
B.	SCs		
1.	Bauri (Agricultural labourer)	9	0.95
2.	Dhoba (Washerman)	10	0.95
3.	Hadi (Nightsoil remover)	105	9.92
4.	Kandara (Village watchman)	12	1.13
5.	Keuta (Fisherman)	14	1.32
6.	Kumbhara (Potter)	7	0.66
7.	Pana (Toddy brewer)	22	2.08
8.	Sundhi (Alcohol brewer)	4	0.38
	Sub-Total	*183*	*17.30*
C.	STs		
1.	Bathudi	1	0.95
2.	Ho	1	0.95
3.	Kolha	198	18.71

(Contd...)

(1)	*(2)*	*(3)*	*(4)*
4.	Munda	16	1.51
5.	Sabara	5	0.47
6.	Santal	84	7.94
	Sub-Total	*305*	*28.32*
D.	*Un-classified*		
1.	Bihari	10	0.95
2.	Bengali	2	0.19
3.	Muslim	8	0.76
4.	Telugu	87	8.22
5.	Nepali	7	0.66
	Sub-total	*114*	*10.78*
	Total	1058	100.00

Source: Secretary, Patharabandha (as per the survey conducted on 2.11.99)

3

Demographic Background of the Sample Population

Various social components, relating to demography, contribute to different social revelations since one social variable is greatly dependent on the other. Hence, before we discuss about the result of this study, we must now deal with some important demographic aspects of the ethnic groups that have been studied. As mentioned in the introductory chapter, the ethnic groups studied are: Brahman from the upper caste Hindu social order, Chasa from the middle caste Hindu social order and Bauri and Santal from the lower social order. A total number of 50 households from each of these ethnic groups have been taken as sample and the result is based on the answers of the population falling in these households.

Distribution of Ethnic Groups by Population, Age and Sex

Data relating to the sample ethnic groups and their population size according to age and sex are presented in Table 4.1. It is revealed that from amongst these 4 ethnic groups, the Chasa people have highest number of population, i.e. 265 as compared to the Bauri (247), Brahman (246) and Santal (239) people. Of the total population of each community, the proportion of male members is found to be higher than those of the female members in all the communities excepting the Brahman. (There are 52.08 per cent of males as against 47.92 per cent females of Chasa community. In Bauri community the proportion of females is only 44.53 per cent as to 55.44 percentage of males and the Santals have 48.12 per cent of females as against 51.88 per cent males). If one looks at the data available in the grand total column, the trend is also observed to be the same, since out of the whole population of 997, 521 or 52.26 per cent are male and the rest 476 or 47.74 per cent are found to be female members.

Of the total population of each caste community, most of the people irrespective of sex are concentrated in the age group of 10-19 but in case of the Brahman and Santal communities, highest number of females are concentrated in the age group of 20-29, in the rest two communities, viz Chasa and Bauri highest number of males are found in the age group of 10-19.

Distribution of Ethnic Groups according to Educational Status

The educational status of the people belonging to different ethnic groups is presented in Table 3.2. It is revealed from the data available in this table that of the 4 ethnic groups, educationally the Brahman people are the most advanced since as many as 181 or 80.44 per cent of the total 225 (after deduction of population falling in the age group of 0-4) population of this community are found to be literate. They are followed by 131 or 52.10 per cent of Chasa, 96 or 43.24 per cent of Bauri and 84 or 41.58 per cent of Santal people. This otherwise indicates that highest percentage (58.42%) of Santal people are illiterate. Next to them, there are Bauri (56.76%), Chasa (47.60%) and Brahman (19.56%) people who are illiterate. But in all the caste communities, the rate of literacy of female members is found to be much lower than those of the male members. It comes to 69.37 per cent of females as against 91.23 per cent of males in Brahman community, followed by 42.86 per cent of females as against 61.07 per cent males of Chasa community, 28.42 per cent females as against 53.27 per cent males in Santal community and 24.74 per cent of females as against 57.60 per cent of males in Bauri community. However, the total figures signify that of the whole population, irrespective of any caste, there are 65.62 per cent of male members as against only 42.42 per cent of female members who are literate (Table 3.2).

As to the level of education achieved by the literate persons, it can be observed that there is none in Santal community who is a graduate but there are at least some in Chasa (3 or 1.2%) and Bauri (2 or 0.90%) communities who have completed this level of education. On the contrary there are as many as 27 or 12 per cent of graduates and 9 or 4 per cent of master-degree holders among the Brahman community. The educational level of the rest population of all the ethnic groups rests in between lower primary to + 2 level (Table 3.3.).

The educational status of the male and female informants of each ethnic group follows more or less the same trend as of the total population. Hence, in case of all the ethnic groups, viz Brahman, Chasa, Bauri and Santal, the rate of literacy among the female informants is less than the male informants. However, when the highest percentage of female informants (66%) belonging to Brahman community are found to be literate, it is least, i.e. 12 per cent in case of the female informants of Santal community. They are followed by Chasa (32.43%) and Bauri (20%) castes. On the contrary, the male Brahmans report highest percentage of literacy that comes to be 88 per cent. They are followed by 58 per cent of Chasa, 52.60 per cent of Bauri and 42 per cent of Santal male informants who are found to be literate. The total figures show that when 60 per cent of male informants irrespective of any caste are literate, it is only 32.5 per cent in case of the female informants taking all groups together (Table 3.4). The educational level of male and female informants is presented in Table 3.5 which is self explanatory.

Distribution of Households according to Occupation

One's occupation is predominantly determined by its caste membership in rural areas. But due to the advancement in the level of education and modernization, caste norms have more or less become redundant and the people have drifted from their own caste occupations. But it has not yet been possible among the castes of lower social order because of their educational and economic backwardness and fear of social sanctions ordained by God. However, there are some households who have taken to different whitecollar jobs that are not based on their castes. As a result in the present study, various occupations are found to have been taken to by the people of different ethnic groups.

The traditional caste occupation of the Brahman is to worship Gods and render priestly services to other people belonging to the *varna* organisation. The Chasas are the traditional agriculturist caste and the people of Bauri caste are the traditionally agricultural wage-earners and conch-shell blower. They render their ritual service to various people during festive occasions and rituals. The, Santals, being a tribal community did not have any specific occupation rather they were earning their daily bread and butter from their forest as food gathers and hunters and also as swiddeners. But nowadays they are following various jobs, mainly wage-earning. However, the people of these four communities are found to have taken to various occupations that are either caste based or not so.

Of the total 50 sample households from each caste community, the Brahman households earn their livelihood from 7 types of occupation, viz agriculture (31 or 62%), service in public sector institutions (7 or 14%), shop-keeping (3 or 6%), service in private sector institutions (3 or 6%), driving of motor vehicles (1 or 2%), village petty politics, like elected panchayat worker (1 or 2%), and providing medicine to the public as untrained medical practitioners, like, homeopathic quack (1 or 2%). The rest 3 or 6 per cent households earn their daily bread and butter out of their own caste occupation, i.e. by providing priestly service to others and working as traditional cooks during festive occasions. The Chasa households earn their daily bread from 9 types of occupation. These are: agriculture (19 or 38.0%), share-cropping (10.20%), shop-keeping (6 or 12.00%), working in private sector institutions (4 or 8.00%), providing contract labour as petty contractor (3 or 6.00%), vending of vegetables (2 or 4.00%) and wage-earning (2 or 4.00%). The Bauri households have adopted as many as 10 types of occupations, such as, wage-earning preferably agricultural labour (32 or 64.00%), rickshaw/trolly pulling (4 or 8%), coconut plucking (3 or 6.00%), driving of motor vehicles 2 or 4.00%), service in public sector institutions (2 or 4.00%), share-cropping (2 or 4.00%), service in private sector institutions (2 or 4.00%), and tuition (1 or 2.00%). The households of the rest one community, i.e. Santal are found to have chosen 8 types of occupation for their livelihood. These are: wage-earning (26 or 52.00%), masonry (8 or 16.00%), rickshaw/trolly pulling (6 or 12.00%), service in public sector institutions (4 or 8.00%), driving of motor vehicles (2 or 4.00%), shop-keeping (2 or 4.00%), carpentry (1 or 2.00%) and service in private sector institutions (1 or 2.00%). Thus, from the above analysis, it comes to the notice that when most of the households of Brahman and Chasa community earn their daily bread primarily from agriculture, the people of the rest two communities, viz Bauri and Santal mostly depend on wage-earning for managing their households. The second important occupation from which quite a sizeable number of households earn their livelihood, comes to be service in public sector institutions for the Brahmans, share-cropping for the Chasa, rickshaw or trolly pulling for Bauris and masonry work for the Santals (Table 3.6).

Nature of Society and Family Forms

The nature of society is highly influenced by family forms. We may discuss the type and family forms of the sample ethnic groups basing on authority system, lineage, residence of female spouse after marriage and inheritance of surnames by the female spouses and children born to a married couple.

All the four ethnic groups are patriarchal, patrilineal, patrilocal in nature (Table 3.7). As a result, all these communities are also patronymic in nature. There is not a single household in any of the ethnic groups, that signifies to be either matriarchal or matrilineal or matrilocal and thereby matronomic. Hence all the households of each caste, being patriarchal in nature, recognise the authority of male heads since in this type of family, the male family or household head exercises exclusive power in the family. He controls all the family members and his ancestral property. All the family members are considered as subordinate to him and all the subordinates are to respect and obey his orders and wishes, otherwise, the head may initiate action against the deviants.

As in patriarchal families, the father or the eldest male of the household acts as the guardian and the whole familial social system revolves round him, in matriarchal societies, the mother or the eldest female member acts as the head of the family and all others are considered as subordinates to her.

The patriarchal families are patrilineal in nature by which the history of a family is traced through lineage in the male line and the deads are propitiated and the annual *sradha* and other such rituals are performed in this line. Thus, in this type of families the lineage system is known after the name of the father. As a result, the female ancestors are not normally recognised as ritually important as the male ancestors and hence they are not propitiated in patrilineal societies or the annual *sradha* is offered in their favour. On the contrary, in matrilineal families a reverse trend is generally observed.

Since in patriarchal societies, the authority system rests with the father or the eldest male member of the family, and the lineage is known after the name of the father or the eldest male member, the female spouse has to inherit the surname of her husband and the progenies born to the couple are surnamed after the surname of their father. Thus, the patriarchal societies are generally patronymic in nature.

In patrilocal societies, the wife has to leave all her natal relatives and come permanently to reside with her husband and other affines at her husband's house. On the other hand in matrilocal societies, after marriage, the husband has to leave his blood relatives and stay permanently with his wife at her affine's house as among the Khasis, Garos and Gaintia of Meghalaya. But among the *Nayars* of Kerala the husband stays at his natal home and visits his wife for biological reasons. He looks after his married sister's properties and children. Thus, since all the studied ethnic groups are patriarchal, patrilineal, patrilocal and patronymic in nature, the women in these societies do not find an equal status compared to their male counterparts. As a result, they are less frequently consulted in the familial management and provided with less opportunities for education. These, age-old social systems, have no doubt made them backward in various fronts and thus, among all the studied ethnic groups they have remained as an underclass subordinates. However, even though like other communities, the nature of the Santal community is patriarchal, patrilineal, patrilocal and patronymic in nature, the females of this community enjoy some freedom than others as they are more or less economically independent. It happens because of their higher earning ability and more freedom to desert their spouses if there is incompatibility.

Family Type and Ethnic Groups

The data presented in Table 3.8 show that most (22 or 44.00%) of the households of the Brahman community are of vertically extended ones. The other households of this community are of nuclear (19 or 38.00%) and supplemented (9 or 18.00%) type. But in the rest 3 communities, viz Chasa, Bauri and Santal, most of the people live in nuclear type of households. The number of this type of households comes to be 30 (60.00%) for the Chasa, 27 (54.00%) for the Bauri and 35 (70.00%) for the Santal. The other household types are: vertically extended (12 or 24.00%) and supplemented (8 or 16.00%) for the Chasa, vertically extended (13 or 26.00%) and supplemented (10 or 20.00%) for the Bauri and vertically extended (7 or 14.00%) and supplemented (8 or 16.00%) for the Santal. Thus, the total figures show that irrespective of any caste community, highest number of households, i.e. 111 or 55.5 per cent are of nuclear type, 54 or 27.00 per cent are of vertically extended type and the rest 35 or 17.5 per cent are of supplemented type.

Table—3.1: Distribution of population according to age and sex

Age groups	*Brahman*			*Chasa*			*Bauri*			*Santal*			*Total*		
	M	*F*	*T*	*M*	*F*	*T*	*M*	*F*	*T*	*M*	*F*	*T*	*M*	*F*	*T*
(1)	(2)	(3)	(4)	(5)	(6)	(7)	(8)	(9)	(10)	(11)	(12)	(13)	(14)	(15)	(16)
0-4	8 (2.25)	13 (5.28)	21 (8.54)	7 (2.64)	8 (3.02)	15 (5.66)	12 (4.86)	13 (5.26)	25 (10.12)	17 (7.11)	20 (8.37)	37 (15.48)	44 (4.41)	54 (5.42)	98 (9.83)
5-9	10 (4.07)	10 (4.06)	20 (8.13)	15 (5.67)	15 (5.66)	30 (11.32)	20 (8.10)	8 (3.24)	28 (11.34)	19 (7.95)	18 (7.53)	37 (15.48)	64 (6.42)	51 (5.12)	115 (11.53)
10-19	23 (9.35)	24 (9.76)	47 (19.11)	42 (15.85)	42 (15.85)	84 (31.70)	41 (16.60)	27 (10.93)	68 (27.53)	25 (10.46)	21 (8.79)	46 (19.25)	131 (13.14)	114 (11.43)	245 (24.57)
20-29	18 (7.32)	28 (13.8)	46 (18.70)	18 (6.79)	15 (5.66)	33 (12.45)	23 (9.31)	22 (8.91)	45 (18.22)	15 (6.28)	24 (10.04)	39 (16.32)	74 (7.42)	89 (8.95)	163 (16.3)
30-39	24 (9.76)	23 (9.35)	47 (19.11)	19 (7.17)	25 (9.43)	44 (16.60)	10 (4.05)	22 (8.91)	32 (12.96)	24 (10.04)	18 (7.53)	42 (17.57)	77 (7.72)	88 (8.83)	165 (16.35)
40-49	19 (7.72)	11 (4.47)	30 (12.20)	25 (9.43)	16 (6.04)	41 (15.47)	21 (8.5)	10 (4.05)	31 (12.55)	14 (5.86)	10 (4.18)	24 (10.04)	79 (7.92)	47 (4.71)	126 (12.64)
50-59	9 (4.47)	4 (1.63)	13 (4.28)	7 (2.64)	3 (1.13)	10 (3.77)	8 (3.24)	3 (1.21)	11 (4.45)	9 (3.77)	2 (0.84)	11 (4.60)	33 (3.31)	12 (1.20)	45 (4.51)
60 +	11 (4.47)	11 (4.47)	22 (8.94)	5 (1.89)	3 (1.13)	8 (3.02)	2 (0.81)	5 (2.02)	7 (2.83)	1 (0.42)	2 (0.84)	3 (1.26)	19 (1.91)	21 (2.11)	40 (4.01)
Total	122 (49.59)	124 (50.41)	246 (100.00)	138 (52.08)	127 (47.92)	265 (100.00)	137 (55.44)	110 (44.53)	247 (100.00)	124 (51.88)	115 (48.12)	239 (100.00)	521 (52.26)	476 (47.74)	997 (100.00)

Note: Figures in brackets represent % age.

Table—3.2: Total literate and illiterate population according to ethnic groups

Variables	*Brahman*			*Chasa*			*Bauri*			*Santal*			*Total*		
	M	*F*	*T*	*M*	*F*	*T*	*M*	*F*	*T*	*M*	*F*	*T*	*M*	*F*	*T*
(1)	*(2)*	*(3)*	*(4)*	*(5)*	*(6)*	*(7)*	*(8)*	*(9)*	*(10)*	*(11)*	*(12)*	*(13)*	*(14)*	*(15)*	*(16)*
Literate	104 (91.23)	77 (63.37)	181 (80.44)	80 (61.07)	51 (42.86)	131 (52.40)	72 (57.60)	24 (24.74)	96 (43.24)	57 (53.27)	27 (28.42)	84 (41.58)	313 (65.62)	179 (42.42)	492 (54.73)
Illiterate	10 (8.77)	34 (30.63)	44 (19.56)	51 (38.93)	68 (57.14)	119 (47.60)	53 (42.40)	73 (75.26)	126 (56.76)	50 (46.73)	68 (71.58)	118 (58.42)	164 (34.68)	243 (57.58)	407 (45.27)
Total	114 (100.00)	111 (100.00)	225 (100.00)	131 (100.00)	119 (100.00)	250 (100.00)	125 (100.00)	97 (100.00)	222 (100.00)	107 (100.00)	95 (100.00)	202 (100.00)	477 (100.00)	422 (100.00)	899 (100.00)

Note: *(i)* Figures in brackets represent % age.

(ii) Calculation is made after deducting the population falling in the age group of 0-4 from the total population.

Table—3.3: Educational status of total population according to ethnic groups

Educa-tional level	*Brahman*			*Chasa*			*Bauri*			*Santal*			*Total*		
	M	*F*	*T*	*M*	*F*	*T*	*M*	*F*	*T*	*M*	*F*	*T*	*M*	*F*	*T*
(1)	*(2)*	*(3)*	*(4)*	*(5)*	*(6)*	*(7)*	*(8)*	*(9)*	*(10)*	*(11)*	*(12)*	*(13)*	*(14)*	*(15)*	*(16)*
Illiterate	10 (8.77)	34 (30.63)	44 (19.56)	51 (38.93)	68 (57.14)	119 (47.6)	53 (42.4)	73 (75.26)	126 (56.76)	50 (46.73)	68 (71.58)	118 (58.42)	164 (34.38)	243 (57.58)	407 (45.27)
1st-5th	27 (23.68)	18 (16.22)	45 (20.0)	38 (29.01)	19 (15.97)	57 (22.80)	30 (24.0)	15 (15.46)	45 (20.27)	38 (35.51)	23 (24.21)	61 (30.20)	133 (27.88)	75 (17.77)	208 (23.14)
6th-10th	21 (18.42)	24 (21.62)	45 (20.0)	26 (19.85)	20 (16.81)	46 (18.40)	34 (27.2)	8 (8.25)	42 (18.92)	16 (14.95)	4 (4.21)	20 (9.90)	97 (20.34)	56 (13.27)	153 (17.02)
Matri-culate	12 (10.53)	16 (14.41)	28 (12.44)	10 (7.63)	8 (6.72)	18 (7.20)	5 (4.0)	1 (1.03)	6 (2.70)	1 (0.93)	–	1 (0.50)	28 (5.87)	25 (5.92)	53 (5.90)
Inter-mediate	18 (15.79)	7 (6.31)	25 (11.11)	4 (3.05)	3 (2.52)	7 (2.80)	1 (0.8)	–	1 (0.45)	2 (1.87)	–	2 (1.0)	25 (5.24)	10 (2.37)	37 (4.12)
Gradua-tion	16 (14.04)	11 (9.91)	27 (12.00)	2 (1.53)	1 (0.84)	3 (1.20)	2 (1.6)	–	2 (0.90)	–	–	–	20 (4.19)	12 (2.84)	32 (3.56)
Master-degree	8 (7.02)	1 (0.9)	9 (4.0)	–	–	–	–	–	–	–	–	–	8 (1.68)	1 (0.24)	9 (1.00)
Technical	2 (1.75)	–	2 (0.9)	–	–	–	–	–	–	–	–	–	2 (0.42)	–	2 (0.22)
Total	114 (100.00)	111 (100.00)	225 (100.00)	131 (100.00)	119 (100.00)	250 (100.00)	125 (100.00)	97 (100.00)	222 (100.00)	107 (100.00)	95 (100.00)	202 (100.00)	477 (100.00)	422 (100.00)	899 (100.00)

Note: As per Table 3.2.

Table—3.4: Total literate and illiterate population according to ethnic groups

Variable	*Brahman*			*Chasa*			*Bauri*			*Santal*			*Total*		
	M	*F*	*T*	*M*	*F*	*T*	*M*	*F*	*T*	*M*	*F*	*T*	*M*	*F*	*T*
(1)	*(2)*	*(3)*	*(4)*	*(5)*	*(6)*	*(7)*	*(8)*	*(9)*	*(10)*	*(11)*	*(12)*	*(13)*	*(14)*	*(15)*	*(16)*
Literate	44 (88.00)	33 (66.00)	27	29 (58.00)	16 (32.00)		26 (52.00)	10 (20.00)		21 (42.00)	6 (12.00)		120 (60.00)	65 (32.50)	
Illiterate	6 (12.00)	17 (34.00)	23	21 (42.00)	34 (68.00)	55	24 (48.00)	40 (80.00)	64	29 (58.00)	44 (88.00)	73	80 (40.00)	135 (67.50)	215
Total	50 (100.00)	50 (100.00)	100 (100.00)	50 (100.00)	50 (100.00)	100 (100.00)	50 (100.00)	50 (100.00)	100 (100.00)	50 (100.00)	50 (100.00)	100 (100.00)	200 (100.00)	200 (100.00)	400 (100.00)

Note: Figures in brackets represent % age.

Table—3.5: Educational status of informants according to ethnic groups

Educational levels	*Brahman*		*Chasa*		*Bauri*		*Santal*		*Total*	
	Male spouse	*Female spouse*	*Male spouse*	*Female spouse*	*Male spouse*	*Female spouse*	*Male spouse*	*Female spouse*	*Male spouse*	*Female spouse*
(1)	*(2)*	*(3)*	*(4)*	*(5)*	*(6)*	*(7)*	*(8)*	*(9)*	*(10)*	*(11)*
Illiterate	6 (12.00)	17 (34.00)	21 (42.00)	34 (68.00)	24 (48.00)	40 (80.00)	29 (58.00)	44 (88.00)	80 (40.00)	135 (67.50)
1st-5th	4 (8.00)	8 (16.00)	16 (32.00)	7 (14.00)	13 (26.00)	6 (12.00)	5 (10.00)	4 (8.00)	38 (19.00)	25 (12.50)
6th-10th	2 (4.00)	12 (24.00)	9 (18.00)	6 (12.00)	9 (18.00)	3 (6.00)	8 (16.0)	2 (4.00)	28 (14.00)	23 (11.50)
Matriculates	16 (32.00)	7 (14.00)	2 (4.00)	2 (4.00)	1 (2.00)	1 (2.00)	4 (8.00)	–	23 (11.50)	10 (5.00)
Inter-mediate	8 (16.00)	4 (8.00)	1 (2.00)	–	1 (2.00)	–	2 (4.00)	–	12 (6.00)	4 (2.00)
Graduation	10 (20.00)	2 (4.00)	1 (2.00)	1 (2.00)	2 (4.00)	–	2 (4.00)	–	15 (7.50)	3 (1.50)
Master-degree	2 (4.00)	–	–	–	–	–	–	–	2 (1.00)	–
Technical	2 (4.00)	–	–	–	–	–	–	–	2 (1.00)	–
Total	50 (100.00)	50 (100.00)	50 (100.00)	50 (100.00)	50 (100.00)	50 (100.00)	50 (100.00)	50 (100.00)	50 (100.00)	50 (100.00)

Note: Figures in brackets represent % age.

Table—3.6: Distribution of informants according to occupation

Sl. No.	*Occupation*	*Brahman*	*Chasa*	*Bauri*	*Santal*	*Total*
(1)	(2)	(3)	(4)	(5)	(6)	(7)
1.	Agriculture	31 (62.00)	19 (38.00)	–	–	50 (25.00)
2.	Coconut plucking	–	–	3 (6.00)	–	3 (1.50)
3.	Carpenting	–	–	–	1 (2.00)	1 (0.5)
4.	Driving of motor vehicles	1 (2.00)	–	2 (4.00)	2 (4.00)	5 (2.50)
5.	Elected panchayat workers	1 (2.00)	–	1 (2.00)	–	2 (1.00)
6.	Homoeopathic quack	1 (2.00)	–	–	–	1 (0.50)
7.	Masonry	–	2 (4.00)	1 (2.00)	8 (16.00)	11 (5.50)
8.	Petty contractor	–	3 (6.00)	–	–	3 (1.50)
9.	Rickshaw/trolly pulling	–	–	4 (8.00)	6 (12.00)	10 (5.00)

(Contd...)

(1)	(2)	(3)	(4)	(5)	(6)	(7)
10.	Service in public sector institutions	7 (14.00)	2 (4.00)	2 (4.00)	4 (8.00)	15 (7.50)
11.	Share-cropping	–	10 (20.00)	2 (4.00)	–	12 (6.00)
12.	Shop-keeping	3 (6.00)	6 (12.00)	–	2 (4.00)	11 (5.50)
13.	Temporary worker in private sector institutions	3 (6.00)	4 (8.00)	2 (4.00)	1 (2.00)	10 (5.00)
14.	Traditional cook/priest	3 (6.00)	–	–	–	3 (1.50)
15.	Tuition	–	–	1 (2.00)	–	1 (0.50)
16.	Vegetable selling	–	2 (4.00)	–	–	2 (1.00)
17.	Wage-earning	–	2 (4.00)	32 (64.00)	26 (52.00)	60 (30.00)
	Total	50 (100.00)	50 (100.00)	50 (100.00)	50 (100.00)	200 (100.00)

Note: Figure in brackets represent % age.

Table—3.7: Nature of society to ethnic groups (N = 50 for each caste)

Ethnic groups	*Authority*		*Lineage*		*Living place of female spouse after marriage*		*Inheritance of surname*	
	Partiarchal	*Matriarchal*	*Patrilineal*	*Matrilineal*	*Patrilocal*	*Matrilocal*	*Patronymic*	*Matronymic*
(1)	*(2)*	*(3)*	*(4)*	*(5)*	*(6)*	*(7)*	*(8)*	*(9)*
Brahman	50 (100.00)	0	50 (100.00)	0	50 (100.00)	0	50 (100.00)	0
Chasa	50 (100.00)	0	50 (100.00)	0	50 (100.00)	0	50 (100.00)	0
Bauri	50 (100.00)	0	50 (100.00)	0	50 (100.00)	0	50 (100.00)	0
Santal	50 (100.00)	0	50 (100.00)	0	50 (100.00)	0	50 (100.00)	0

Note: Figures in brackets represent % age.

Table—3.8: Family types according to ethnic groups

Family types	*Brahman*	*Chasa*	*Bauri*	*Santal*	*Total*
(1)	*(2)*	*(3)*	*(4)*	*(5)*	*(6)*
Nuclear	19 (38.00)	30 (60.00)	27 (54.00)	35 (70.00)	111 (55.50)
Vertically extended	22 (44.00)	12 (24.00)	13 (26.00)	7 (14.00)	54 (27.00)
Supplemented	9 (18.00)	8 (16.00)	10 (20.00)	8 (16.00)	35 (17.50)
Total	50 (100.00)	50 (100.00)	50 (100.00)	50 (100.00)	200 (100.00)

Note: Figures in brackets represent % age.

Table—3.9: Distribution of households according to *Gotra*/Clan

Sl. No.	*Gotra/Clan*	*Brahman*	*Chasa*	*Bauri*	*Santal*
(1)	*(2)*	*(3)*	*(4)*	*(5)*	*(6)*
1.	*Bharadwaj*	33 (66.00)	–	–	–
2.	*Parasara*	6 (12.00)	–	–	–
3.	*Sankuchya*	10 (20.00)	–	–	–
4.	*Atreya*	1 (2.00)	–	–	–
5.	*Nagasa/Naga*	–	36 (72.00)	5 (10.00)	–
6.	*Kashyap*	–	8 (16.00)	–	–
7.	*Gobardhan*	–	2 (4.00)	–	–
8.	*Surya*	–	2 (4.00)	–	–
9.	*Sankha*	–	2 (4.00)	–	–
10.	*Laxman (Hati)*	–	–	45 (90.00)	–

(Contd...)

(1)	(2)	(3)	(4)	(5)	(6)
11.	*Khandajanga*	–	–	–	11 (22.00)
12.	*Karama*	–	–	–	7 (14.00)
13.	*Champa*	–	–	–	10 (20.00)
14.	*Neem*	–	–	–	6 (12.00)
15.	*Put*	–	–	–	2 (4.00)
16.	*Sal*	–	–	–	1 (2.00)
17.	*Miru*	–	–	–	7 (14.00)
18.	*Raseek*	–	–	–	4 (8.00)
19.	*Bari*	–	–	–	2 (4.00)
	Total	50 (100.00)	50 (100.00)	50 (100.00)	50 (100.00)

Note: Figures in brackets represent % age.

Cultural Milieu

Educational and Socio-Economic Deprivation of the Girl Child and the Woman

Culture and the Notion of Sex Preference in Birth

Various social characteristics and the cultural set practices are very much responsible for determination of social status of male and female individuals. As a result, since we do not have similar type of human societies everywhere in the world, the social status of men and women differs much from one society to another depending upon the nature of such societies and the cultural practices prevailing among the people therein. It has already been discussed in earlier chapters, that the social status of men in comparatively high as compared with the women in patriarchal societies wherein the authority of the father or the eldest male member of the family is solely recognised and lineage is traced in his line. Moreover, the locality of residence of the female spouse changes to the house of her husband or any other affinal relative and even the surname of the female spouse is changed according to the surname of her husband. The legitimate children born to her are also required to be known after the surname of her husband or the father of the children. As a matter of fact, in such societies, the male head remains as the sole authority overall the ancestral properties and all such properties are inherited by the male children but not by female children. Thus, in a society which is patriarchal in nature, both type of female members, viz the female spouses and the female children do not enjoy an equal status with their male counterparts rather in all respects they are treated as subordinates or as underclass members in the family. And in most of the cases, in this type of societies, the female children are considered as social and economic burden on the parents. What is more surprising is that, in this type of societies, even a mother does not prefer a female child and if such a child is born to her, she may treat it as an inauspicious event. This happens not because by nature she is biased or cruel towards her female children, rather she behaves negatively since she is socialised in such a society or cultural milieu.

In the context of the foregoing discussions, in the present study an attempt has been made to find out if there is practically any such discrimination prevailing among the four communities studied. The result, certainly sprouts some amazing revelations. In order to assess the present social status of the girl children in the families of Brahman, Chasa, Bauri and Santal communities, several direct and indirect questions (Appendix: 1) were put to the presents. First of all when a question relating to the 'desired sex' for their first issue was put, most of them opined for a boy child. Specifically, highest percentage of Bauri (94%) households followed by 86 per cent of Santal, 84 per cent of Chasa and 76 per cent of Brahman households opined that they had wanted a male issue. Exceptionally, only 4 or 8 per cent of Brahman households and 1 or 2 per cent of Bauri households said that they had intended to have female issues. The rest households of each community did not have any choice (Table 4.1).

The households which opined that they should have girl children, adduced that begetting the first issue as a girl child is an auspicious event and an indicator of prosperity for the family. But the households that had no choice of sex, opined that since determination of sex of a child is divinely ordained and the man cannot do anything against it, they should not have any choice over it. If God wishes, it would give a male child, otherwise a female one. So, one must get satisfied with what God gives in the form of a child.

The households which had desired to have male issues, pointed out as many as 6 multiple factors in order to justify their desires. Of these factors, economic importance of male children observed to be the most vital reason behind opting for a boy child as in all the communities, most of the people, viz 76.74 per cent of Santal, 72.34 per cent of Bauri, 71.43 per cent of Chasa, and 71.5 per cent of Brahman households consider a male child as an economic assets. This, otherwise, means that these households consider a girl child as an economic burden on them. The next important factor is found to be 'old-age security' has been highlighted by 23 or 53.49 per cent of Santal, 21 or 44.68 per cent of Bauri and 13 or 30.95 per cent of Chasa people. But for the Brahmans, the second most important factor comes to be 'fulfillment of ascribed ritual assignments' since 19 or 50 per cent of informants of this community argue in its favour. However, if one looks at the data available in the total column, it is found that irrespective of any community, of the total 170 households that wanted male children, a total number of 124 or 72.94 per cent households point out economic importance of male children as the basic and foremost reason behind their desire for a male child. The next important reason is observed to be 'old-age security' as this factor has been focussed by a total number of 72 or 42.35 per cent of households. 'Old-age security' has been highlighted in the sense that either the male children or their spouses would be helpful to them during their old-age. Apart from them, the grandchildren would also equally be helpful during their old-age. The daughters may not be able to render this essential help to their parents during their old-age since as per the custom of the society, they leave their parent's house after their marriage and permanently stay at the home of their husbands. They visit their parents occasionally or on some special occasions as relatives. Hence, no parent can demand the service of its married daughters during his/her old-age. Another reason behind opting for boy children is that the male children have many ritual responsibilities to perform, as for example, the eldest male child is required to offer some amount of holy water of the *ganga* river in the mouth of his parents at their dying moments and give *mukhagni,* (funeral pyre) to them after their death. Otherwise, it is believed that the soul of the dead would not get *Mukti* or *Mundane* salvation. Hence, the soul of the dead parents remain dissatisfied and therefore their spirits might become malevolent and thus cause problems for the family. Next to this point, a total number of 33 or 19.41 per cent households asserted that it is essential that one should have at least one male child in order to save and continue one's own agnatic line and hence inherit and protect the parental properties. Interestingly, 10 or 5.58 per cent households categorically revealed a fact that if one gets a male child as its first issue, it would help the couple to limit the size of its family. Otherwise, the couple has to go in for procreating the next child with a hope to have a male issue. And, if the second issue is still a female one, the process of procreation does not stop until a male issue is begotten. This, ultimately leads to creation of a large family and subsequently it becomes a great economic burden for the parents. So, if the first issue is a male child then it means, it would fulfil all the expected social, ritual and economic duties of the family. As a result, one may stop procreation of more children after having a male child (Table 4.2).

Apart from asking about the desired sex of the first child, a subsequent question relating to gender discrimination, i.e. the total number of children a married couple should have and the sexual division thereof was put to the same informants in order to assess their mentality on gender biasness at the familial level. The result of this question is presented in Table 4.3, 4.4 (a), 4.4 (b), 4.4 (c) and 4.4 (d).

Table 4.3. indicates that highest percentage of Santal, Brahman and Bauri people say that a couple should have at least 2 children, but of the total 50 sample households of each community, a total number of 35 or 70 per cent of Santal households say this, it is 24 or 48 per cent for the Brahman and 44 or 28 per cent for the Bauri households. Maximum, i.e 19 or 38 per cent of Chasa households opine that a couple should have at least 3 children. However, the total figures revealed that of the total households of all the 4 communities, there are only 15 or 7.50 per cent of households who opine that a couple should have only one child as against 94 or 47 per cent of households who say that it should have minimum 2 children. The households who opt for 3 children per couple account for a total number of 54 households which is 27 per cent of the total sample size. Again quite a good number of households, i.e. or 10.5 per cent are there who say that the concerned number be 4 per couple and the households who want that a couple should have as many as 5, 6, 7 and 8 children account for 1 or 0.5 per cent, 3 or 1.5 per cent, 2 or 1 per cent and 3 or 1.5 per cent respectively. The rest 7 or 3.5 per cent households answered differently as they opine that they are not sure about the number of children a couple should have, since the number of children a couple gets is predetermined and man cannot do anything either to reduce or to increase the number according to its own wish. Absolutely it depends on the Almighty. If one goes against this natural set practice through any artificial method the result may be detrimental.

Of the total number of children desired, the parents, wanted at least one male child, are more than those wanted at least one female child per couple. However, among the Brahman households a total number of 48 or 96 per cent households wanted male children as against only 36 or 72 per cent who wanted female children. There are 2 (4%) households who have no choice of any sex for their progenies before they were born [Table 4.4 (a)].

Among the Chasa, Bauri and Santal people, there are 48 or 97.87 per cent, 44 or 95.65 per cent and 48 or 96 per cent of households respectively who want that each of them should have at least one boy child. The rest households did not have any choice over sex. The households who wanted at least one girl child account for 32 or 68.09 per cent for the Chasa, 33 or 71.74 per cent for the Bauri and 36 or 72 per cent for the Santal [Table 4.4 (b)], [Table 4.4 (c)] and [Table 4.4 (d)]. However, the average number of boy and girl children opted for begetting per household shows an amazing revelation. When in each of the communities, the average number of boy children wanted is about 2 per family, it is less than 1 girl child.

Educational Deprivation and the Girl Child

Education is an important aspect in the life of all individuals irrespective of sex. In countries where formal education has reached more people, it is comparatively more developed than those where people are less literate. More particularly where more females are educated, the socio-economic development of that country is more satisfactory. Because, if a female is educated, it is considered that a family is educated and if a male is educated, it is thought that only one person is educated. This is because of the fact that the women remain in charge of the household duties including looking after the children. If she is educated, automatically the children and other family members become educated and accordingly their awareness and worldview also increase. But in Indian traditional patriarchal societies, the women have not been provided with formal education since long past because of the age-old inherent social practices and the prevailing social prejudices. As a result, the proportion of educated females to the educated males has remained much lower, even though, nowadays, their rate of literacy is increasing steadily. Still then the overall rate of literacy of women in traditional casteist societies is much lower as compared to their male counterparts. This is also witnessed from the findings of the present study.

In order to find out the level of literacy among the male and female children and the reasons associated with their illiteracy, three important age groups, viz 5-9, 10-19 and 20-21 have been formulated in which people normally attain formal education.

Of the total 42 male Brahman population falling in these 3 age groups, 39 or 92.86 per cent of them are found to be literate as against 23 or 63 per cent of females of the total 36 female population of these 3 age groups. But when of the total literate male population, as many as 30 or 76.92 per cent are continuing their education in different classes, it is only 16 or 69.56 per cent of females who are now studying. The rest male and female population have either discontinued their study after completing certain levels of education or are dropouts [Table 4.5 (a)].

Table 4.5 (b)] shows that there are 67 male and 68 female members belonging to the Chasa community in the said age groups. Of these total population, 46 or 68.66 per cent of male as against 29 or 42.65 per cent of females are observed to be literate. But when of the total literate male members, more than 76 per cent are continuing their education, there are only 16 or 55.17 per cent of females who do this. Similarly the trend is also same for the rest two communities, viz Bauri and Santal but the gap of literacy between male and female members of these two communities is very high compared to the male and female population of Brahman and Chasa communities. However, when of the total 74 Bauri male population, the literate people account for a total number of 57 or 77.03 per cent, it is merely 19 or 38.78 per cent of females of this community and the rest people are found to be illiterate. It is also further observed from the same table that when of the total literate male population, presently about 58 per cent of 33 persons are continuing their education, it is only about 37 per cent of 7 females who are found to be doing so [Table 4.5 (c)].

So far as the case of the Santal people is concerned, it is witnessed that of the total 54 male and 53 female population, 31 or 57.41 per cent males and 18 or 33.96 per cent females are literate and the rest are all illiterate. But the percentage of male population who are now continuing education is found to be very high (64.52) as compared to the respective percentage (27.78) of the female population [Table 4.5 (d)].

Thus, from the above findings it is observed that in all the communities the rate of literacy of females is much lower than their male counterparts.

However, in order to find out gender discrimination in respect of availing an educational opportunity, some questions relating to a probable situation was put to the informants. The probable situation and the related questions were as follows: 'suppose you have 4 children, 2 sons and 2 daughters and government wants to provide free education with all other facilities, like, boarding and lodging free of cost only to 2 of them. In that case whom do you select from amongst your 4 children?' Surprisingly most of the Santal (33 or 66%), Chasa (31 or 62%), Bauri (27 or 54%), households opted to avail such an opportunity for both of their sons as against a total number of 21 or 42 per cent of Brahman households who also wanted this. All the rest households opted to avail the said opportunity for one boy and one girl child. Surprisingly there was none among any of the communities that opted to avail the opportunity in favour of both their girl children (Table 4.6).

The above findings certainly indicate that in the matter of availing educational opportunities, the girl children are not favoured by most of the households of the traditional societies. However, in order to discern whether practically the households which chose one boy and one girl for the said programme of the government, give equal importance to their boy and girl children, a subsequent question was also put. The question was related to the provision of employment for only one of the two educated children after completion of education under the said scheme. In that case when about 79 per cent of Chasa people opted for availing this opportunity in favour of their boy children, it was 76.47 per cent of the Santal, 73.91 per cent for the Bauri and 65.57 per cent for the Brahman households who also gave a similar opinion. The rest households, however, opined that they would prefer such an employment opportunity for any child whoever is found fit and qualified better than the other (Table 4.7). Thus, it becomes perspicuous that in all the 4 communities, the girl children remain deprived of their basic rights to education and also employment at the household level. Since educationally they are discriminated against the boy children at the familial level, in later stage of their life they find themselves very helpless and unable to enter into the job markets because of their illiteracy. This certainly compels them to remain under their male counterparts, both educationally as well as economically.

Factors Responsible for Illiteracy among Girl Child and Women

In order to find out the factors responsible for illiteracy, the total illiterate persons and the population who are dropouts or have discontinued their education after completion of certain level of education have been added up together. And the total figures obtained thereof in different age groups have been taken as 'N' (Table 4.8).

The factors responsible for illiteracy among the male and female population of different communities are observed to be as many as 13 in number (Table 4.9). Of these, 3 factors are exclusively related to different classroom problems and personal academic career. Two are concerned with illness or health problems of self and other family members or death of their parents and the rest 8 factors are social and economic in nature. All these factors came out into the fore as multiple answers. As a result, each factor does not seem to be an independent variable that is solely responsible for reducing the level of literacy either among the male children.

However, so far as the factors responsible for illiteracy among the male and female persons are concerned, it can be said that for the Brahman community, the most important factor responsible for illiteracy of male children is found to be failure in class promotion examinations as this factor is pointed out by a total number of 4 or 33.33 per cent of households. But on the contrary, the most important factor that has caused reduction in the level of literacy among female children is found to be the poor economic condition of their parents. However, among all the rest 3 communities, viz Chasa, Bauri and Santal, poor economic condition of parents is found responsible as the most important reason of spreading illiteracy among both the male and female children. But what is amazing is that even though highest percentage of people belonging to these communities assert that their poor economic condition does not permit them to educate their male and female children, there are more parents who point out this reason as the most important and striking aspect for reducing the level of literacy among their female children but the gap between the percentage of parents who have said that this factor is the most important factor for illiteracy among their male children and those who have advocated that this factor is responsible for the persistence of illiteracy among their female children is very big in case of all the four communities.

The Brahman households, who have pointed out their poor economic condition as an important reason of illiteracy among their male children, account for 25 per cent or 3 households as against 40 per cent or 8 households who have remarked this being the most radical factor for lowering literacy among the female members. Similarly 40.62 per cent or 13 Chasa households say that their poor economic condition does not permit them to educate their male children, there are as high as 50 per cent or 26 households who focussed this as the prime reason for not sending their girl children to educational institutions. Further, when about 59 (58.54) per cent Bauri households say that they are basically wage-earners and hence are not able to educate their male children, there are as high as 74 per cent or 31 households who have held this factor being responsible for higher rate of illiteracy among their female children. The Santal are also of the same view but when a total number of 18 or 52.94 per cent of them identify their poverty being the prime cause of illiteracy among their male children, there are as many as 30 or 62.5 per cent of households who point out this as the most important reason for their female children being illiterates.

From the above findings, an important point comes to the fore. It can certainly be said that the same parents cannot be poor for educating their girl children and well-to-do for the male children. But it is observed that when in many cases the same parents say that they are not educating their girl children because of their poor economic condition, at the same time they are sending their male children to school. This practice continues for an important social factor. They feel that spending money on the education of female children means wasting their scarce resources they have, since, in traditional patriarchal societies, the female children are considered as the wealth of others as they leave their parents and reside permanently with their affines at their in-law's house after their marriage and if in that case an educated girl gets employed, her income goes directly to the family fund of her husband but never comes to the hand of her parents. If at all it comes, it comes occasionally as gift or loan. Again, it may also occur for three other important social reasons. First of all, in patriarchal societies, after marriage, a girl, is considered as the property of her husband or of her affines and in that case, her husband and parents-in-law remain as her sole guardian or authority and custodian of what she earns either as an employed person or as a wage-earner or as an entrepreneur. Secondly, after marriage, a girl considers her husband, children and some of her close affines as her close relations with whom she has to lead her whole life. She takes to this sort of attitude as a result of her socialisation. The society also demands this sort of attitude and behaviour. The norms of the society compel her to exhibit manifest indifference towards her consanguines and thus, under social compulsion she remains under such a state of mind. In other words, she remain helpless and unable to do anything for her parents beyond certain prescribed limits. The third important factor is that, traditionally the women are treated as if they are born to manage the home front, like cooking daily-food for the family members and serve it properly to them and looking after the children. Hence, there is no need for them to go to school and get educated as the male children who are supposed to earn and financially support the family. So, the poor people do not like to spend their scarce resources on the education of their female children rather spend the same for educating their male children who are supposed to remain for while of their lifetime with their parents. They would get employed after completion of their education and hence would be socially as well as financially helpful to their parents during their old-age.

However, if one looks at the data available in the total column of the same table, it may be seen that poor economic condition of parents remains as the most important factor of illiteracy among the male as well as female children irrespective of any community. But when this factor is attributed to be a cause of illiteracy for about 49 per cent or 58 male children, it is about 59 per cent or 95 for female children. The second most important factor in order of numerical strength is observed to be the disinterest of parents to spend money on the education of female children. As has already been pointed out earlier, it happens because the female children leave their parents after their marriage and reside with their husbands. And unemployment among 16 young man (13.45%) works as negative factor against education of male children in some cases. Some parents say that there are many educated unemployed young men in their society. So, there is also no guarantee that their male children would get employment after their education. It necessitates the parents not to spend their hard-earned money on the education of their male children, who would remain outside the pale of job-market.

Helping parents in different economic and day-to-day household pursuits is an important reason which is rated as the third important reason for illiteracy of both the male and female children since this point has been highlighted for 30.25 per cent or 49 girl children as against the same percentage of male children. The male children normally help their fathers in agricultural activities and the girls help their mothers in various households duties, like sweeping the house floor and backyards, cleaning of utensils and washing of clothes, fetching water from water resources for their daily consumption etc.

Apart from the above factors, there are three more factors which exclusively remain behind reducing the literacy level among the female children. These reasons are: (i) attaining of adulthood or marriageable age by the girls (47 or 29.01%, (ii) problem of finding out educated spouse for the educated girls (28 or 17.28%), and (iii) general negative attitude of society (8 or 4.94%). These factors come out as the 3rd, 6th and 9th important causes respectively in chronological order of importance for persistence of illiteracy among the girl children.

Among the traditional casteist and economically poor patriarchal societies attainment of adulthood by the girls is considered as attainment of marriageable age, and once a girl gets matured means it becomes a headache for the parents. They concentrate their attention on the preparation for marriage of such girl children, rather than on their education. Even in some cases the parents stop education of these girl children. Once they get matured, parents advise them to learn the art of cooking and other such household activities from their mothers or from any other senior female members of the family seriously since these aspects are traditionally considered as the basic required knowledge for the girl children to get married. If a girl is perfect in cooking and household management, her life becomes smooth and easy otherwise simply possession of formal educational degrees does not help her to achieve love and affection of her husband or other affines. Moreover, the parents feel that once a girl gets highly educated means it creates problems for them as they are to search for a matching groom who is more qualified than their daughter, and in such a case, the poor parents may not be able to meet the amount of dowry demanded by the groom's party. Thus, such a situation may compel some parents to search for a groom who is less qualified than their daughters. But if such a marriage proposal is solemnised, the familial life of the married couple gets disturbed. Because in a male dominated society, the male members, particularly, the husbands want that in all respects they should always remain dominant over their female counterparts. And the women, themselves desire that their life-partners must be more educated and hence earn more than them. So, in order to avoid this sort of unpleasantness, the poor parents remain cautious and do not like to educate their daughters more, and therefore, hesitate to provide higher education to their daughters.

Looking after younger siblings during the absence or even during the working hours of parents, particularly mothers, in the fourth important factor behind the illiteracy of female children. This activity is specific to the female sex based on the norms of sexual division of labour. However, exceptionally male children are also engaged in this work but their percentage of engagement in this activity is less than the opposite sex. As a result, when this factor comes in the fourth order for the female children, it ranks in the seventh position amongst the factors responsible for lowering the rate of literacy among the male children. Another important factor that seems to be similar to the above one but practically it is distinct by its own characters. This factor is: 'engagement of female children in different economic pursuits at an early age, i.e. at school-going age. This factor has been pointed out for 20.99 per cent of female children as against 20.17 per cent of 24 male children. Hence, this factor ranks in the 5th and 3rd order amongst all the factors pointed out for female and male children respectively. The female children are generally engaged as maid servant and the boys are forced to work as rag-pickers, petty vendors, assistants in garages and roadside shanty hotels etc. in order to economically support their parents. The other factors found responsible for the illiteracy or dropout or discontinuance of education among females are based on the health problems of self (4 or 2.42%) and family planning, like parents (23 or 14.20%), and on some other fields, like failure in class promotion examinations (12 or 7.14%), fear of school teachers (3 or 1.85%) and poor academic career (3 or 1.85%) which does not facilities admission of such children to higher educational levels, like availing of college education or any other such education. The corresponding figures for the males are found to be 8 or 6.72 per cent, 12 or 10.08 per cent, 14 or 11.76 per cent, 19 or 15.97 per cent, and 4 or 3.36 per cent respectively.

Culture of Dining and the Women

In each and every society 'food' occupies a pivotal place in the daily life of all the individuals irrespective of age and sex since it has various symbolic, ritual and physical significance in relation to its preparation, sharing and consumption by the family members. As a symbolic element of culture, most often it is very intrinsically involved with the social status of female members as both in patriarchal as well as in matriarchal societies, the attitude and the social role of such members, particularly female spouses, is very important in relation to preparation of food and serving food items among all the family members. This food-culture involves various social norms and regulations as to who should prepare, when, how and at what time it should be served and to whom it should be served first and the persons who should eat last and how the surplus food or even the leftovers be used.

Preparation of food and distribution of it among the family members is normally done by women since this work is gender specific as per the prevailing societal norms of sexual division of labour. Moreover, at the same time it is also a natural process by which women become mothers and as such they become more attached to their progenies. This compels them to collect or prepare food for their children so that they could survive. But certainly she is not responsible for any other members as per the law of the nature. Still then, in human societies, they remain absolutely responsible to prepare food and serve this to all the family members, like, parents-in-law, husband, children and other members if there are any. However, in order to enable her to discharge her duty properly, men look after it by the way of providing ration or any other such materials required for cooking and serving food to the family members. As a social practice this work is undertaken by men and the women remain in-charge of kitchen and food preparation.

What is actually surprising is that women, particularly the female spouse prepare daily-food but normally they cannot consume the same before it is served to their male counterparts and children or any other senior male members of the family. This happens mainly because traditionally women consider their husbands as prototype of god, and want to earn ritual merits by doing so. On the contrary most of the husbands also want their respective spouses must behave in this manner. The grown up girls follow their mothers and prepare themselves for their future role in their respective husband's houses after marriage. The present study also supports these views. However, it does not happen in all the cases since there are several households who do not follow this age-old practice of the society. This might be due to the impact of modernization and higher awareness among such households.

In this context, Table 4.10 indicates that 86 per cent or 43 Chasa households say that in their families the male and female members do not sit together for lunch/supper even during the availability of all the family members at home. The corresponding figures for Brahman, Bauri and Santal people are: 84, 74 and 62 per cent respectively. All these households together account for 76.5 per cent of the total figure and the rest households of each community maintain that both the male and female members of their families sit together for taking lunch or super. However, of the total households (47) who say that all of them irrespective of sex sit together for lunch/supper during availability of all the family members, 63.83 per cent or 30 households opine that they do so frequently and there are 23.40

per cent or 11 households who follow this practice occasionally and the rest 12.77 per cent of households sit together for lunch/ supper very occasionally [4.10 (a)]. However, the households, in which all the male and female members do not sit together for lunch/supper, the male spouses and male children are normally served food first [Table 4.10 (b)] and the female spouses and female children take food after the male members have their lunch/supper. [Table 4.10 (c)]. However, in these households, there is no restriction for younger girl children who may take their food with their fathers or elder brothers or any other senior male members of the family. But once the girls are grown up, it means they must wait until their father or elder brothers have finished their lunch/supper. The grown up girls wait so that they can consume the leftover of their fathers or elder brothers as a result no food is wasted by the way of throwing out the leftovers or by providing these to the animals. Another factor is that this system shows the love and devotion of wives towards their husbands, mothers towards their children, daughters towards their fathers, and sisters towards their elder brothers and by doing this, the female spouses earn ritual merits that may be helpful for them to have *mukti* or mundane salvation after their death. However, the Brahmans who are more orthodox than any other caste Hindus or tribal people, have a special ritual practice that indirectly compels the female spouses and the daughters to take food after the male members have consumed. As per the traditional belief, *Arna* (food or literally cooked rice) is considered as *Laxmi* or goddess of wealth. So, it cannot be wasted in any form. If it is done so, then one may lose its property and hence starve to death. Befalling of this misfortune is inevitable. But, there is every possibility that an adult male person may not consume the whole amount of food served to him and hence there may be some leftover and in that case normally the daughters are left as the suitable ones to consume that. One may say that the male children can also consume that but practically it does not happen so since in this community generally the younger boys aging 5, 7 or 9 years undergo sacred thread ceremony or *bratopanayan*; and once a boy undergoes this rite and wears a sacred thread, he has to lead a rigid lifestyle by which he performs *chalu*, a ritual that concerns offering of food to *Brahma*, the creator of the universe, before eating that food. So, as the leftover food of someone cannot be offered to the said deity and children who have undergone the said ritual abstain from eating of such food, more possibility for consuming of such food remains for the daughters than such sons. Another aspect involved in this is that, a male person may require some additional food while eating but if all the male and female members sit together, there would not be anybody to serve the additional food. Moreover, one may not touch the main hearth while eating. If it is touched, the container and the food therein may be polluted. These factors normally compel the lady members to wait and consume food after the male ones are served and have eaten their food.

There are more number of Bauri (26%) and Santal (38%) households than Chasa (14%) and Brahman (18%) who say that all of their family members sit together and eat their food. They opine that they are primarily wage-earners. So, both the husband and wife go out of home during the day time and come back at evening. Hence, they do not have any scope to obey the tradition. The female spouses equally feel tired and hungry with their husbands after coming back home at evening. Still then they are to cook food for the evening. They sit together to take supper in order to save fuel and take rest as early as possible. The Chasa and Brahman households sit together for their lunch/supper, if they are either young couples with younger children or there is no senior family member who could be factor to restrain them from doing so. They say that, had there been any such member in their family, it would not have been possible for them to do so.

Health, Disease and the Process of Treatment

All the living creatures including the human beings are subjected to suffer from various diseases depending on their age and living condition. There are some diseases that occur basing on one's sex. However, these are to be medically treated otherwise the health condition of the sufferers, deteriorates which may cause death of the patient. But in traditional caste Hindu or in some tribal societies equal importance is not given on the health condition of both the male and female members. Particularly in patriarchal societies where the females are considered as an underprivileged class, the women remain deprived of their health facilities apart from many other deprivations they traditionally suffer from. In many cases, due importance is not given to the health condition of women unless they are very serious. This happens for various age-old traditional reasons. In such societies, the parents prefer that the scarce money available with them be spent for the treatment of the male members since they are the bread-winners of the family and once they fall ill means the whole family-economy would get shattered. So, they must be provided with better medical facility so that they can bring the economy of their family to the manageable condition. Apart from this, the diseased women, particularly the spouses, want that the available money preferably be spent for curing their diseased husbands. They prefer so partly because of their love towards their husbands and partly because it would help them to earn ritual merits. These ideas are transferred to the minds of the girl children through the process of socialisation by which they also behave similarly after they are married.

In the above context, data available in Table 4.11, 4.12, 4.13 and 4.14 may be referred to. Table 4.11 depicts that of the total number of 521 male and 476 female members of all the four communities, as many as 135 (25.91%) males as against 113 (23.75%) females are now suffering from at least one disease. But more number of Santal and Bauri men and women are suffering as compared to their counterparts in Chasa and Brahman communities. Because these people are exposed to very unhygienic living conditions and their level of awareness on personal health and hygiene in comparatively poor than others. Apart from this, their poor economic condition also does not permit them to protect themselves from certain diseases by the way of using antiseptic ointments or using mosquito nets or even keeping themselves neat and clean.

A perusal of Table 4.12 makes it clear that highest percentage of Bauri (46.15%), Santal (40.18%), and Chasa (22.22%) males suffer from cold and cough as against highest number of Chasa (40%), Santal (34.21%) and Bauri females who are also suffering from this disease. Among the Brahmans, when maximum male (6 or 33.33%) suffer from viral fever, highest percentage (36.36) of females suffer from cold and cough. If one looks at the total figures, it comes to the notice that of the total 135 diseased male, a total number of 45 (33.33%), suffer from cold and cough. They are followed by those who suffer from viral fever (30.37%), gastric problem (11.85%), scabies (11.85%), joint pain (9.63), conjunctivitis/ophthalmia (8.15%), waist/back pain (6.67%), whitlow (6.67%), abdominal pain (5.19%), asthma (4.44%), itching (3.70%), would on body (3.70%), headache, piles (2.96%), high blood pressure (2.96%), blister (1.48%), earache (1.48%), filaria (1.48%), malaria (1.48%), collic (0.74%), diarrhoea (0.74%), jaundice (0.70%) and low blood pressure (0.70%).

So far as the case of the females is concerned, highest percentage (35.40%) of them suffer from cold and cough (35.40%). The other diseases from which the rest of the females suffer are: itching (26.55%), viral fever (26.55%), scabies (18.58%), abdominal pain (15.93%), conjunctivitis/ophthalmia (14.16%), joint pain (12.39%), whitlow (9.73%), would on body and feet (8.85%), earache (5.31%), gastric problem (4.42%), piles (4.42%), waist/back pain (4.42%), asthma (2.65%), headache (1.77%), low blood pressure (1.77%), malaria (1.77%), diarrhoea (0.88%), dog-bite (0.88%), high blood pressure (0.88%) and measles (0.88%).

Even though less number of male and female members of Brahman community are suffering from various diseases as compared to their counterparts of other communities, more number of male and female patients of this community are undergoing medical treatment for curing their ailments. This is because they are financially more sound and educationally more advanced than the Santal, Bauri and Chasa people. However, it is very peculiar to observe that in all these 4 communities more number of male patients are now under medical treatment than their female counterparts. This trend certainly indicates that the females are deprived of their health care. So far as the statistical figures are concerned, of the total 18 Brahman patients, as many as 14 or 77.78 per cent are presently undergoing medical treatment. They are followed by the Chasa (63.88%), Santal (52.38%), and Bauri (43.58%), patients who are undergoing such treatment. Similarity when there are 63.64 or 14 female Brahman patients, there are 27.27 per cent or 9 Bauri, 31.58 per cent or 12 Santal and 52.38 per cent or 10 female Chasa patients, who are undergoing medical treatment (Table 4.13). Apart from these patients, there are some male and female patients who are undergoing treatment under the local traditional medicinemen or shamans who normally sit in trans for identifying the supernatural cause of ailment and prescribe appropriate rituals or traditional medicines which may or may not have any proper medicinal importance. Still then the patients or family members keep deep faith on this and get cured either because of their psychological satisfaction or because of the medicinal impact of the herbs prescribed by such healers. Normally the tribals have more faith on this either because of their age-old tradition or because of their simplicity and low level of awareness. Again, this method of treatment normally involves less financial expenditure. As a result, more number of tribal patients opt for this rather than going to modern hospitals and have medicine therefrom. The aforesaid table also shows some data relating to the number of patients undergoing this treatment. It is found that there are more number of Santal male and female patients than such patients among the Bauri and Chasa communities who are undergoing treatment under this method. But there is none in the Brahman community who is observed to be undergoing this sort of treatment. However, when there are 7 or 16.17 per cent of Santal, 7 or 21.21 per cent of Bauri and 2 or 10 per cent of Chasa female patients who are under the treatment of various traditional medicinemen or shamans, the rest patients are not undergoing any treatment rather they are to simply put up with the disease because of their poor economic condition.

So far as the type of treatment among the patients who are undergoing modern medical treatment is concerned, it is found that highest number of male and female patients of each community are undergoing allelopathic treatment followed by those who are undergoing homeopathic and ayurbedic treatments. When a total number of 50 male patients irrespective of any community accounting for 65.79 per cent of the total 76 patients are using allopathic medicine, there are 24 or 53.33 per cent of female patients undergoing this treatment. Next to these patients there are 4 or 33.33 per cent of male and 23 or 30.26 per cent of female patients using homeopathic medicines. There are only 3 or 3.95 per cent of male patients undergoing ayurbedic treatment (Table 4.14).

Allopathic medicines are costly but the impact of this medicine is immediately observed on the patient. On the other hand, homeopathic medicines are very cheap but its impact on the patient is not immediately observed as like allopathic medicines. Still then a sizable number of male and female patients use this medicine either because they are poor or because they have deep faith on this medicine. Ayurvedic medicine are also equally costly like those of allopathic medicines. Therefore, there are very few patients who are found to be using this medicine. However, when comparatively more number of male patients are using allopathic medicines, there are more female patients who are under homeopathic treatment.

Occupation, Utilisation of Income and the Level of Exploitation of Labour

Occupation of a person greatly depends on its caste and sex. However, since nowadays the caste norms have been very flexible in urban fringes, many do not consider those and have taken to various white-collar and other similar jobs depending upon their own choice, interest, educational qualification and profitability of such jobs as a number of such modern jobs are open for all irrespective of gender. Still then, a major chunk of the caste Hindu women belonging to the upper strata of the social order have not yet come forward to avail such job opportunities and earn for themselves or for their family members. As a result, they have still remained as housewives but most of them belonging to the lower castes and tribal communities work as wage-earners and supplement their family income. Now, let us examine how the wages of the employed women is utilised. It must be found out whether they have ownership right over their own earnings or their husbands usurp such right on that. In this context, one may refer to the data available in Tables 4.15, 4.16 and 4.17.

A perusal of Table 4.15 signifies that of the total of 200 cases, as many as 107 or 53.50 per cent of female spouses are housewives, followed by 85 or 42.5 per cent who are wage-earners and there are 7 or 3.5 per cent of women who run some petty business in order to supplement their family income. The rest 1 or 0.5 per cent woman is a service-holder. However, when there are 98 and 92 per cent of female spouses among the Brahman and Chasa communities respectively who are housewives and as such are engaged in housekeeping activities, there are only 10 per cent of such Bauri and 14 per cent of Santal women who are exclusively engaged in this work. These women do not earn any money as ready cash since their work does not provide this. On the contrary as high as 86 per cent of Bauri and 82 per cent of Santal women are engaged in wage-earning in different sectors. The rest 6 per cent of Chasa, 4 per cent of Bauri and also Santal women are running some petty business, like shop-keeping and vending of edible items. There is only one Brahman woman who is a salaried service holder. All these persons more or less earn some ready cash. But more than 59 per cent of them say that the whole amount earned by them is handed over to their respective husbands as against about 40 per cent of them who say that they keep all their earnings with self and also receive the earnings of their husbands in order to manage their families. But certainly they do so as per the wish of their husbands (Table 4.16).

The only one Brahman female spouse, who is a service-holder, says that even if she earns a good amount of money as her salary, she lacks occupancy right on it since she has to give a major part of it to her husband and keep the minor part with self to meet her daily necessities, like meeting bus fare, taking some tiffins during office hour or meeting any other such basic requirements in her office (Table 4.16). But even if she earns, she stresses that she cannot purchase a major item either for herself or for any of her relatives or even for any of her own family members without the prior permission of her husband.

The female spouses do not spend the money earned by themselves and have to spend the money as per the wish of their spouses or give it to them. Of the total 93 cases, as many as 78 (83.87%) informants say that their husbands take it by force otherwise their social life gets disturbed. While doing so, many husbands use vulgar languages against their wives or even beat them to justify their lordship over them. If any wife agitates against this act of her husband, she is threatened to get divorced. This, of course, makes her mum since she lacks any other permanent and suitable alternative than to tolerate or to remain as such with her husband in such an adverse social situation. Hence, she has to resist all the negative behaviour of her husband and thus, she leads a very bitter life with intense mental tension and tranquility of mind. In this context, the data presented in the said table shows that there are as many as 17 or 18.28 per cent of female spouses who are threatened to get divorced by their husbands. However, there are 7 or 7.53 per cent of earning female spouses who opine that nothing negative happens to them if they keep their own earnings with themselves. But certainly they are to spend that for the general welfare of the family members of their husbands (Table 4.17).

Table—4.1: Desired sex of the first child among different ethnic groups

Ethnic groups	*Boy child*	*Girl child*	*No option*	*Total*
(1)	(2)	(3)	(4)	(5)
Brahman	33 (76.00)	4 (8.00)	8 (16.00)	50 (100.00)
Chasa	42 (84.00)	–	8 (16.00)	50 (100.00)
Bauri	47 (94.00)	1 (2.00)	2 (4.00)	50 (100.00)
Santal	43 (86.00)	–	7 (14.00)	50 (100.00)
Total	170 (85.00)	5 (2.5)	25 (12.5)	200 (100.00)

Note: Figures in brackets represent % age.

Table—4.2: Factors responsible for opting a boy child as the eldest progeny

Sl. No.	*Factors*	*Brahman*	*Chasa*	*Bauri*	*Santal*	*Total*
(1)	*(2)*	*(3)*	*(4)*	*(5)*	*(6)*	*(7)*
1.	Economic support to father	27 (71.05)	30 (71.43)	34 (72.34)	33 (76.74)	124 (72.94)
2.	Fulfillment of ritual requirements	19 (50.00)	7 (16.67)	6 (12.77)	5 (11.63)	37 (21.76)
3.	Old-age security	15 (39.47)	13 (30.95)	21 (44.68)	23 (53.49)	72 (42.35)
4.	To continue generation	10 (26.32)	4 (9.52)	8 (17.02)	11 (25.58)	33 (19.41)
5.	To remain free from dowry and marriage problems of daughters	4 (10.53)	–	–	–	4 (2.25)
6.	To limit family	4 (10.53)	3 (7.14)	3 (6.38)		10 (5.88)

Note: Figures in brackets represent % age.

Table—4.3: No. of children a couple should have

Ethnic group	No. of children 1	2	3	4	5	6	7	8	Not sure	Total
(1)	(2)	(3)	(4)	(5)	(6)	(7)	(8)	(9)	(10)	(11)
Brahman	3	24	19	4	–	–	–	–	–	50
	(6.00)	(48.00)	(38.00)	(8.00)						(100.00)
Chasa	6	14	19	5	–	1	1	1	3	50
	(12.00)	(28.00)	(38.00)	(10.00)		(2.00)	(2.00)	(2.00)	(6.00)	(100.00)
Bauri	3	21	8	9	1	2	–	2	4	50
	(6.00)	(42.00)	(16.00)	(18.00)	(2.00)	(4.00)		(4.00)	(8.00)	(100.00)
Santal	3	35	8	3	–	–	1	–	–	50
	(6.00)	(70.00)	(16.00)	(6.00)			(2.00)			(100.00)
Total	15	94	54	21	1	3	2	3	7	200
	(7.50)	(47.00)	(27.00)	(10.50)	(0.50)	(1.50)	(1.00)	(1.50)	(3.50)	(100.00)

Note: Figures in brackets represent % age.

Table—4.4 (a) Option for boy and girl children among Brahman households

No. of children a couple should have	*Total HHs opted*	*Total no. of children*	*No. of HHs opted for boy children*	*% age to total HHs opted*	*Total no. of boy children*	*% age to total children*	*No. of HHs opted for girl children*	*% age to total HHs opted*	*Total no. of girl children*	*% age to total children*	*HHs having no option for sex*	*% age to total HHs*	*Total children of any sex*	*% age to total children*
(1)	*(2)*	*(3)*	*(4)*	*(5)*	*(6)*	*(7)*	*(8)*	*(9)*	*(10)*	*(11)*	*(12)*	*(13)*	*(14)*	*(15)*
1.	3 (6.00)	3	2	66.67	2	66.67	–	–	–	–	1	33.33	1	33.33
2.	24 (48.00)	48	23	95.83	30	62.5	16	66.67	16	33.33	1	4.17	2	4.17
3.	19 (38.00)	57	19	100.00	39	68.42	16	84.21	18	31.58	–	–	–	–
4.	4 (8.00)	16	4	100.00	11	68.67	4	100.00	5	31.25	–	–	–	–
Total	50 (100.00)	124	48	96.00	82	66.13	36	72.00	39	31.45	2	4.00	3	2.42

Note: Figures in brackets represent % age.

Table—4.4 (b) Option for boy and girl children among Chasa households

No. of children a couple should have	Total HHs opted	Total no. of children	No. of HHs opted for boy children	% age to total HHs opted	Total no. of boy children	% age to total children	No. of HHs opted for girl children	% age to total HHs opted	Total no. of girl children	% age to total children	HHs having no option for sex	% age to total HHs	Total children of any sex	% age to total children
(1)	(2)	(3)	(4)	(5)	(6)	(7)	(8)	(9)	(10)	(11)	(12)	(13)	(14)	(15)
1.	6 (12.77)	6	6	100.00	6	100.00	–	–	–	–	–	–	–	–
2.	14 (29.79)	28	13	92.86	15	53.57	10	71.43	10	35.71	1	7.14	2	7.14
3.	19 (40.43)	57	19	100.00	42	73.68	14	73.68	16	28.07	–	–	–	–
4.	5 (10.64)	20	5	100.00	12	60.00	5	100.00	8	40.00	–	–	–	–
5.	–	–	–	–	–	–	–	–	–	–	–	–	–	–
6.	1 (2.13)	6	1	100.00	4	66.67	1	100.00	2	33.33	–	–	–	–
7.	1 (2.13)	7	1	100.00	6	85.71	1	100.00	1	14.29	–	–	–	–
8.	1 (2.13)	8	1	100.00	7	87.50	1	100.00	1	12.5	–	–	–	–
Total	47 (100.00)	132	46	97.87	92	69.70	32	68.09	38	28.79	1	2.13	2	1.52

Note: (i) Figures in brackets represent % age.
(ii) 3 households out 50 sample household did not specified the no. of children a couple should have.

Table—4.4 (c): Option for boy and girl children among Bauri households

No. of children a couple should have	Total HHs opted	Total no. of children	No. of HHs opted for boy children	% age to total HHs opted	Total no. of boy children	% age to total children	No. of HHs opted for girl children	% age to total HHs opted	Total no. of girl children	% age to total children	HHs having no option for sex	% age to total HHs	Total children of any sex	% age to total children
(1)	(2)	(3)	(4)	(5)	(6)	(7)	(8)	(9)	(10)	(11)	(12)	(13)	(14)	(15)
1.	3 (6.52)	3	·3	100.00	3	100.00	–	–	–	–	–	–	–	–
2.	21 (45.65)	42	20	95.24	25	59.52	15	71.43	15	35.71	1	4.76	2	4.76
3.	8 (17.39)	24	8	100.00	17	70.83	7	87.50	7	29.17	–	–	–	–
4.	9 (19.57)	36	8	88.89	24	66.67	7	77.78	8	22.22	1	11.11	4	11.11
5.	1 (2.17)	5	1	100.00	5	100.00	–	–	–	–	–	–	–	–
6.	2 (4.35)	12	2	100.00	9	75.00	2	100.00	3	25.00	–	–	–	–
7.	–	–	–	–	–	–	–	–	–	–	–	–	–	–
8.	2 (4.35)	16	2	100.00	11	68.75	2	100.00	5	31.25	–	–	–	–
Total	46 (100.00)	138	44	95.65	94	68.12	33	71.74	38	27.54	2	4.35	6	4.35

Note: Figures in brackets represent % age.

Table—4.4 (d): Option for boy and girl children among Santal households

No. of children a couple should have	*Total HHs opted*	*Total no. of children*	*No. of HHs opted for boy children*	*% age to total HHs opted*	*Total no. of boy children*	*% age to total children*	*No. of HHs opted for girl children*	*% age to total HHs opted*	*Total no. of girl children*	*% age to total children*	*HHs having no option for sex*	*% age to total HHs*	*Total children of any sex*	*% age to total children*
(1)	(2)	(3)	(4)	(5)	(6)	(7)	(8)	(9)	(10)	(11)	(12)	(13)	(14)	(15)
1.	3 (6.00)	3	3	100.00	3	100.00	7	–	–	–	–	–	–	–
2.	35 (70.00)	70	33	94.29	38	54.29	26	74.29	28	40.40	2	5.71	4	5.71
VB 3	8 (16.00)	24	8	100.00	16	66.67	8	100.00	8	33.33	–	–	–	–
4.	3 (6.00)	12	3	100.00	6	50.00	2	66.67	6	50.00	–	–	–	–
5.	–	–	–	–	–	–	–	–	–	–	–	–	–	–
6.	–	–	–	–	–	–	–	–	–	–	–	–	–	–
7.	1 (2.00)	7	1	100.00	7	100.00	–	–	–	–	–	–	–	–
Total	50	116	48	96.00	70	60.34	36	72.00	42	36.21	2	4.00	4	3.45

Note: (*i*) The average in 'a' column has been worked out from those who opted boy or girl children and the average in 'b' column has been worked out from the total population.

(*ii*) Figures in brackets represent % age.

Table—4.5 (a): Education among Brahman households according to broad age groups and sex

Age groups	Total population		Illiterate		Literate males			Literate females		
	M	F	M	F	Conti-nuing	Disconti-nuing	Total	Conti-nuing	Disconti-nuing	Total
(1)	(2)	(3)	(4)	(5)	(6)	(7)	(8)	(9)	(10)	(11)
5-9	10 (100.00)	10 (100.00)	–	4 (40.00)	10 (100.00) (100.00)	–	10 (100.00) (100.00)	6 (60.00) (60.00)	–	6 (60.00) (100.00)
10-19	23 (100.00)	24 (100.00)	–	7 (25.00)	15 (65.22) (65.22)	8 (34.28) (34.78)	23 (100.00) (100.00)	10 (41.67) (58.82)	7 (29.17) (41.18)	17 (70.83) (100.00)
20-24	9 (100.00)	2 (100.00)	3 (33.33)	2 (100.00)	5 (55.56) (83.33)	1 (11.11) (16.67)	6 (66.67) (100.00)	–	–	–
Sub-total	42 (100.00)	36 (100.00)	3 (7.14)	13 (36.11)	30 (71.43) (76.92)	9 (21.43) (23.08)	39 (92.86) (100.00)	16 (44.44) (69.56)	7 (19.44) (30.43)	23 (63.89) (100.00)
25 +	72 (100.00)	75 (100.00)	7 (9.72)	20 (26.67)	–	65 (90.8) (100.00)	65 (90.28) (100.00)	–	55 (73.37) (100.00)	55 (73.33) (100.00)
Total	114 (100.00)	111 (100.00)	10 (8.77)	34 (30.63)	30 (26.32) (28.85)	74 (64.91) (71.15)	104 (91.23) (100.00)	16 (14.41) (20.51)	62 (55.86) (79.49)	78 (70.27) (100.00)

Note: Figures in brackets represent % age.

Table—4.5 (b): Education among Chasa households according to broad age groups and sex

Age groups	*Total population*		*Illiterate*		*Literate males*			*Literate females*		
	M	*F*	*M*	*F*	*Conti-nuing*	*Disconti-nuing*	*Total*	*Conti-nuing*	*Disconti-nuing*	*Total*
(1)	*(2)*	*(3)*	*(4)*	*(5)*	*(6)*	*(7)*	*(8)*	*(9)*	*(10)*	*(11)*
5-9	15 (100.00)	15 (100.00)	4 (26.67)	11 (73.33)	11 (73.33) (100.00)	–	11 (73.33) (100.00)	4 (26.67) (100.00)	–	4 (26.67) (100.00)
10-19	42 (100.00)	42 (100.00)	11 (26.19)	21 (50.00)	21 (50.00) (67.74)	10 (23.81) (32.26)	31 (73.81) (100.00)	11 (26.19) (52.28)	10 (23.81) (47.61)	21 (50.00) (100.00)
20-24	10 (100.00)	11 (100.00)	6 (60.00)	7 (63.64)	3 (30.00) (75.00)	1 (10.00) (25.00)	4 (40.00) (100.00)	1 (63.64) (25.00)	3 (27.27) (75.00)	4 (36.36) (100.00)
Sub-total	67 (100.00)	68 (100.00)	21 (31.34)	39 (57.35)	35 (52.24) (76.09)	11 (16.42) (23.01)	46 (68.66) (100.00)	16 (23.53) (55.17)	13 (19.12) (44.63)	29 (42.65) (100.00)
25 +	64 (100.00)	51 (100.00)	30 (46.88)	29 (56.86)	–	34 (53.13) (100.00)	34 (53.13) (100.00)	–	22 (43.14) (100.00)	22 (43.14) (100.00)
Total	131 (100.00)	119 (100.00)	51 (38.93)	68 (57.14)	35 (26.72) (43.75)	45 (34.35) (56.25)	80 (61.67) (100.00)	16 (13.45) (31.37)	35 (29.41) (68.63)	51 (42.86) (100.00)

Note: Figures in brackets represent % age.

Table—4.5 (c): Education among Bauri households according to broad age groups and sex

Age groups	*Total population*		*Illiterate*		*Literate males*			*Literate females*		
	M	*F*	*M*	*F*	*Conti-nuing*	*Disconti-nuing*	*Total*	*Conti-nuing*	*Disconti-nuing*	*Total*
(1)	*(2)*	*(3)*	*(4)*	*(5)*	*(6)*	*(7)*	*(8)*	*(9)*	*(10)*	*(11)*
5-9	20 (100.00)	8 (100.00)	3 (15.00)	4 (50.00)	11 (55.00) (64.71)	6 (30.00) (35.29)	17 (85.00) (100.00)	3 (37.5) (75.00)	1 (12.5) (25.00)	4 (50.00) (100.00)
10-19	41 (100.00)	27 (100.00)	8 (19.51)	15 (55.56)	21 (51.22) (63.64)	12 (29.27) (36.36)	33 (80.49) (100.00)	4 (14.81) (33.33)	8 (29.53) (66.62)	12 (44.44) (100.00)
20-24	13 (100.00)	14 (100:00)	6 (46.15)	11 (78.57)	1 (7.7) (14.29)	6 (46.15) (85.71)	7 (53.85) (100.00)	–	3 (21.43) (100.00)	3 (21.43) (100.00)
Sub-total	74 (100.00)	49 (100.00)	17 (22.97)	30 (61.22)	33 (44.59) (57.89)	24 (32.43) (42.11)	57 (77.03) (100.00)	7 (14.29) (36.84)	12 (24.49) (63.16)	19 (38.78) (100.00)
25 +	51 (100.00)	48 (100.00)	36 (70.59)	43 (89.58)	–	15 (29.41) (100.00)	15 (29.41) (100.00)	–	5 (10.42) (100.00)	5 (10.42)
Total	125 (100.00)	97 (100.00)	53 (42.40)	73 (75.26)	33 (26.4) (45.83)	39 (31.20) (54.17)	72 (57.6) (100.00)	7 (7.22) (29.17)	17 (17.53) (70.83)	24 (24.74)

Note: Figures in brackets represent % age.

Table—4.5 (d): Education among Santal households according to broad age groups and sex

Age groups	*Total population*		*Illiterate*		*Literate males*			*Literate females*		
	M	*F*	*M*	*F*	*Conti-nuing*	*Disconti-nuing*	*Total*	*Conti-nuing*	*Disconti-nuing*	*Total*
(1)	*(2)*	*(3)*	*(4)*	*(5)*	*(6)*	*(7)*	*(8)*	*(9)*	*(10)*	*(11)*
5-9	19 (100.00)	18 (100.00)	6 (31.58)	12 (66.67)	10 (52.63) (76.92)	3 (15.79) (23.08)	13 (68.42) (100.00)	2 (11.11) (33.33)	4 (22.22) (66.67)	6 (33.33) (100.00)
10-19	25 (100.00)	21 (100.00)	13 (52.00)	16 (76.10)	7 (28.00) (58.33)	5 (20.00) (41.67)	12 (48.00) (100.00)	3 (14.29) (66.00)	2 (9.52) (40.00)	5 (23.81) (100.00)
20-24	10 (100.00)	14 (100.00)	4 (40.00)	7 (50.00)	3 (30.00) (50.00)	3 (30.00) (50.00)	6 (60.00) (100.00)	–	7 (50.00) (100.00)	7 (50.00) (100.00)
Sub-total	54 (100.00)	53 (100.00)	23 (42.59)	35 (66.64) (64.52)	20 (37.04) (35.48)	11 (20.37) (100.00)	31 (57.41) (27.78)	5 (9.43) (72.22)	13 (24.53) (100.00)	18 (33.96)
25 +	53 (100.00)	42 (100.00)	27 (50.94)	33 (78.57)	–	26 (49.06) (100.00)	26 (49.06) (100.00)	–	9 (21.43) (100.00)	9 (21.43) (100.00)
Total	107 (100.00)	95 (100.00)	50 (46.73)	68 (71.58)	20 (8.69) (35.09)	37 (34.58) (64.91)	57 (53.27) (100.00)	5 (5.26) (18.52)	25 (26.32) (92.59)	27 (28.42) (100.00)

Note: Figures in brackets represent % age.

Table—4.6: Option for availing educational opportunities among different communities

Ethnic groups	*Total HHs*	*Both boys*	*Both girls*	*One boy and one girl*
(1)	*(2)*	*(3)*	*(4)*	*(5)*
Brahman	50	21 (42.00)	–	29 (58.00)
Chasa	50	31 (62.00)	–	19 (38.00)
Bauri	50	27 (54.00)	–	23 (46.00)
Santal	50	33 (66.00)	–	17 (24.00)
Total	100	112 (56.00)	–	88 (44.00)

Note: Figures in brackets represent % age.

Table—4.7: Option for availing opportunity for employment among different communities

Ethnic groups	*N*	*Boys*	*Anyone who studies better*
(1)	*(2)*	*(3)*	*(4)*
Brahman	29 (100.00)	19 (65.52)	10 (34.48)
Chasa	19 (100.00)	15 (78.95)	4 (21.05)
Bauri	23 (100.00)	17 (73.91)	6 (26.09)
Santal	17 (100.00)	13 (76.47)	4 (23.53)
Total	88 (100.00)	64 (72.73)	24 (27.27)

Note: Figures in brackets represent % age.

Table—4.8: Total illiterates and dropouts according to ethnic groups and sex

Ethnic groups	*Total population*		*Total illiterate and dropout students*	
	M	*F*	*M*	*F*
(1)	*(2)*	*(3)*	*(4)*	*(5)*
Brahman	42 (100.00)	36 (100.00)	12 (28.57)	20 (55.56)
Chasa	67 (100.00)	68 (100.00)	32 (47.76)	52 (47.06)
Bauri	74 (100.00)	49 (100.00)	41 (55.41)	42 (85.71)
Santal	54 (100.00)	93 (100.00)	34 (62.96)	48 (90.57)
Total	237 (100.00)	206 (100.00)	119 (50.21)	162 (78.64)

Note: Figures in brackets represent % age.

Table—4.9: Factors responsible for illiteracy and dropout among male and female members of different ethnic groups

Sl. No.	Factors	Brahman		Chasa		Bauri		Santal		Total rank			Rank
		M (N=12)	F (N=20)	M (N=32)	F (N=52)	M (N=41)	F (N=42)	M (N = 34)	F (N=48)	M (N=119)	F (N=162)		
(1)	(2)	(3)	(4)	(5)	(6)	(7)	(8)	(9)	(10)	(11)	(12)	(13)	(14)
1.	Attaining adulthood/ marriageable age	–	3 (15.00)	–	6 (11.54)	–	17 (40.48)	–	21 (43.75)	–		47 (29.01)	3
2.	Diseased parents/ death of parents	2 (16.67)	2 (10.00)	3 (9.38)	7 (13.46)	6 (14.63)	9 (19.05)	1 (2.94)	6 (12.5)	12 (10.08)	8	23 (14.20)	7
3.	Engagement in economic pursuits at an early age	2 (16.67)	–	1 (3.13)	2 (3.85)	8 (19.51)	6 (14.29)	13 (38.24)	26 (54.17)	24 (20.17)	3	34 (20.99)	5
4.	Failure in class promotion	4 (33.33)	3 (15.00)	3 (9.38)	3 (5.77)	2 (4.88)	6 (14.29)	5 (14.71)		14 (11.76)	6	12 (7.41)	8
5.	Fear to teachers	2 (16.67)	–	8 (25.00)	–	6 (14.63)	–	3 (8.82)	3 (6.25)	19 (15.97)	4	3 (1.85)	10
6.	Helping parents in economic/households pursuits	3 (25.00)	6 (30.00)	12 (37.5)	11 (21.15)	13 (31.71)	21 (50.00)	8 (23.53)	11 (22.92)	36 (30.25)	2	49 (30.25)	2
7.	Illness of self	1 (8.33)	–	3 (9.38)	1 (1.92)	3 (7.32)	1 (2.38)	1 (2.94)	2 (4.17)	8 (6.72)	9	4 (2.47)	11

(Contd...)

(1)	(2)	(3)	(4)	(5)	(6)	(7)	(8)	(9)	(10)	(11)	(12)	(13)	(14)
8.	Looking after younger siblings	–	2 (10.00)	–	9 (17.31)	4 (9.76)	18 (42.86)	9 (26.47)	17 (35.42)	13 (10.92)	7	46 (28.40)	4
9.	Poor academic career	3 (25.00)	2 (100.00)	1 (3.13)	1 (1.92)	–	–	–	–	4 (3.56)	10	3 (1.85)	10
10.	Poor economic condition of parents	3 (25.00)	8 (40.00)	13 (40.62)	26 (50.00)	24 (58.54)	31 (73.81)	18 (52.94)	30 (62.5)	58 (48.74)	1	95 (58.64)	1
11.	Problem of searching educated spouse	–	5 (25.00)	–	9 (17.31)	–	6 (14.29)	–	8 (16.67)	–		28 (17.28)	6
12.	Society does not permit/ no body educates	–	–	–	–	–	8 (19.05)	–	–	–		8 (4.94)	9
13.	Unproductive expenditure	1 (8.33)	7 (35.00)	3 (9.38)	6 (11.54)	5 (12.20)	18 (42.86)	7 (20.59)	18 (37.5)	16 (13.45)	5	49 (30.25)	2

Note: Figures in brackets represent % age.

Table—4.10: Do all the male and female members of your family sit together for lunch/supper during the availability of all members?

Answers	*Brahman*	*Chasa*	*Bauri*	*Santal*	*Total*
(1)	*(2)*	*(3)*	*(4)*	*(5)*	*(6)*
Yes	8 (16.00)	7 (14.00)	13 (26.00)	19 (38.00)	47 (23.50)
No	42 (84.00)	43 (86.00)	37 (74.00)	31 (62.00)	153 (76.50)
Total	50 (100.00)	50 (100.00)	50 (100.00)	50 (100.00)	200 (100.00)

Note: Figures in brackets represent % age.

Table—4.10 (a): Frequency of sitting together for lunch/supper among households who sit together for lunch/supper during availability of all members

Frequency	*Brahman (N = 8)*	*Chasa (N = 7)*	*Bauri (N = 13)*	*Santal (N = 19)*	*Total (N = 47)*
(1)	*(2)*	*(3)*	*(4)*	*(5)*	*(6)*
Frequently	3 (37.5)	3 (42.86)	10 (76.92)	14 (73.68)	30 (63.83)
Occasionally	3 (37.5)	2 (28.57)	2 (15.38)	4 (21.05)	11 (23.40)
Very occasionally	2 (25.0)	2 (28.57)	1 (7.69)	1 (5.26)	6 (12.77)

Note: Figures in brackets represent % age.

Table—4.10 (b): Persons served food first among households in which male and female persons do not sit together for lunch/supper

Persons/ % age	*Brahman (N = 42)*	*Chasa (N = 43)*	*Bauri (N = 37)*	*Santal (N = 31)*	*Total (N = 153)*
(1)	*(2)*	*(3)*	*(4)*	*(5)*	*(6)*
Male spouse/ male children	42	43	37	31	153
Percentage	100.00	100.00	100.00	100.00	100.00

Note: Figures in brackets represent % age.

Table—4.10 (c): Persons served food last among households in which male and female persons do not sit together for lunch/supper

Persons/ % age	*Brahman (N = 42)*	*Chasa (N = 43)*	*Bauri (N = 37)*	*Santal (N = 31)*	*Total (N = 153)*
Female spouse/ female children	42	43	37	31	153
Percentage	100.00	100.00	100.00	100.00	100.00

Note: Figures in brackets represent % age.

Table—4.11: Number of male and female persons suffering from atleast one disease

Variables	*Brahman*		*Chasa*		*Bauri*		*Santal*		*Total*	
	M	*F*	*M*	*F*	*M*	*F*	*M*	*F*	*M*	*F*
(1)	*(2)*	*(3)*	*(4)*	*(5)*	*(6)*	*(7)*	*(8)*	*(9)*	*(10)*	*(11)*
Suffering	18 (14.75)	22 (17.74)	36 (26.09)	20 (15.75)	39 (28.47)	33 (30.00)	42 (33.87)	38 (33.04)	135 (25.91)	113 (23.74)
Not suffering	104 (88.25)	102 (82.26)	102 (73.91)	107 (84.25)	98 (71.53)	77 (70.00)	82 (66.13)	77 (66.96)	386 (74.09)	363 (76.26)
Total	122 (100.00)	124 (100.00)	138 (100.00)	127 (100.00)	137 (100.00)	110 (100.00)	124 (100.00)	115 (100.00)	521 (100.00)	476 (100.00)

Note: Figures in brackets represent % age.

Table—4.12: Name of the diseases/ailments from which male and female persons are suffering

Sl. No.	Disease	Brahman		Chasa		Bauri		Santal		Total	
		M (N = 18)	F (N = 22)	M (N = 36)	F (N = 20)	M (N = 39)	F (N = 33)	M (N = 42)	F (N = 38)	M (N = 135)	F (N = 113)
(1)	(2)	(3)	(4)	(5)	(6)	(7)	(8)	(9)	(10)	(11)	(12)
1.	Abdominal pain	–	–	3 (8.33)	6 (30.00)	3 (7.69)	6 (18.18)	1 (2.38)	3 (7.89)	7 (5.19)	18 (15.93)
2.	Asthma	1 (5.56)	–	3 (8.33)	2 (10.00)	1 (2.56)	1 (3.03)	1 (2.38)	–	6 (4.44)	3 (2.65)
3.	Blister	–	–	–	–	–	– (4.26)	2	– (1.48)	2	–
4.	Collic	–	–	1 (2.78)	–	3	–	–	–	1 (0.74)	–
5.	Cold & cough	2 (11.11)	8 (36.36)	8 (22.22)	8 (40.00)	18 (46.15)	11 (33.33)	17 (40.48)	13 (34.21)	45 (33.33)	40 (35.40)
6.	Conjunctivitis/ Ophthalmia	3 (16.67)	4 (18.18)	3 (8.33)	3 (15.00)	2 (5.13)	6 (18.18)	3 (7.14)	3 (7.89)	11 (8.15)	16 (14.16)
7.	Diarrhoea	–	–	–	–	–	1 (2.03)	1 (2.38)	–	1 (0.74)	1 (0.88)
8.	Dog bite	–	–	–	–	–	–	–	1 (2.63)	–	1 (0.88)

(Contd...)

(1)	(2)	(3)	(4)	(5)	(6)	(7)	(8)	(9)	(10)	(11)	(12)
9.	Ear ache	–	2 (9.09)	–	–	2 (5.13)	3 (9.09)	–	1 (2.63)	2 (1.48)	6 (5.31)
10.	Filaria	1 (5.56)	–	–	–	31 (2.56)	–	–	–	2 (1.48)	–
11.	Gastric	1 (5.56)	–	4 (11.11)	2 (10.00)	4 (10.26)	–	7 (16.67)	3 (7.89)	16 (11.85)	5 (4.42)
12.	Headache	–	–	2 (7.72)	1 (5.00)	–	1 (3.03)	2 (4.76)	–	4 (2.96)	2 (1.77)
13.	High blood pressure	3 (16.67)	–	–	1 (5.00)	–	–	1 (2.38)	–	4 (2.96)	1 (0.88)
14.	Itching	–	–	2 (7.72)	8 (40.00)	2 (5.13)	10 (30.3)	1 (2.76)	12 (31.58)	5 (3.70)	30 (26.55)
15.	Jaundice	–	–	–	–	1 (2.56)	–	–	–	1 (0.74)	–
16.	Joint pain	–	–	3 (8.33)	–	3 (7.69)	6 (18.18)	7 (16.67)	8 (21.05)	13 (9.63)	14 (12.39)
17.	Low blood pressure	1 (5.56)	1 (4.55)	–	1 (5.00)	–	–	–	–	1 (6.74)	2 (1.77)
18.	Malaria	–	–	–	–	–	–	2 (4.76)	2 (5.26)	2 (1.45)	2 (1.77)

(Contd…)

(1)	(2)	(3)	(4)	(5)	(6)	(7)	(8)	(9)	(10)	(11)	(12)
19.	Measles	–	–	–	–	–	1 (3.03)	–	–	–	1 (0.88)
20.	Piles	2 (11.11)	2 (9.09)	2 (7.72)	–	–	3 (9.09)	–	–	4 (2.96)	5 (4.42)
21.	Scabies	–	–	3 (8.33)	3 (15.00)	8 (20.51)	7 (21.21)	5 (11.90)	11 (28.95)	16 (11.85)	21 (18.58)
22.	Viral Fever	6 (33.33)	7 (31.82)	4 (11.11)	5 (25.00)	18 (46.15)	6 (18.18)	13 (30.95)	12 (31.58)	41 (30.37)	30 (26.55)
23.	Waist back pain	4 (22.22)	3 (13.64)	2 (7.72)	1 (5.00)	2 (5.13)	–	1 (2.38)	1 (2.63)	9 (6.67)	5 (4.42)
24.	Whitlow	–	–	2 (7.72)	3 (15.00)	6 (15.38)	6 (3.03)	1 (2.38)	7 (18.42)	9 (6.67)	11 (9.73)
25.	Wound on feet and body	–	–	1 (2.78)	–	2 (5.13)	7 (21.21)	2 (4.76)	3 (7.89)	5 (3.70)	10 (8.85)

Note: Figures in brackets represent % age.

Table—4.13: Treatment of the diseased male and female persons

Variables	*Brahman*		*Chasa*		*Bauri*		*Santal*		*Total*	
	M	*F*	*M*	*F*	*M*	*F*	*M*	*F*	*M*	*F*
(1)	*(2)*	*(3)*	*(4)*	*(5)*	*(6)*	*(7)*	*(8)*	*(9)*	*(10)*	*(11)*
Undergoing medical treatment	14 (77.78)	14 (63.64)	23 (63.88)	10 (50.00)	17 (43.58)	9 (27.27)	22 (52.38)	12 (31.58)	76 (56.30)	45 (39.82)
Undergoing other treatment	–	–	3 (8.33)	2 (10.00)	6 (15.38)	7 (21.21)	7 (16.17)	11 (29.95)	16 (11.85)	20 (17.70)
Not undergoing any treatment	4 (22.22)	8 (36.36)	10 (27.78)	8 (40.00)	16 (41.03)	17 (51.52)	13 (30.95)	15 (39.47)	43 (31.85)	48 (42.48)
Total	18 (100.00)	22 (100.00)	36 (100.00)	20 (100.00)	39 (100.00)	33 (100.00)	42 (100.00)	38 (100.00)	135 (100.00)	113 (100.00)

Note: Figures in brackets represent % age.

Table—4.14: Type of treatment among the diseased male and female persons who are undergoing medical treatment

Variables	*Brahman*		*Chasa*		*Bauri*		*Santal*		*Total*	
	M	*F*	*M*	*F*	*M*	*F*	*M*	*F*	*M*	*F*
(1)	*(2)*	*(3)*	*(4)*	*(5)*	*(6)*	*(7)*	*(8)*	*(9)*	*(10)*	*(11)*
Allopathic	9 (64.29)	8 (57.14)	17 (73.91)	5 (50.00)	11 (64.71)	3 (33.33)	13 (59.09)	8 (66.67)	50 (65.79)	24 (53.33)
Ayurvedic	2 (14.29)	–	1 (4.35)	–	–	–	–	–	3 (3.95)	–
Homeopathic	3 (21.43)	6 (42.86)	5 (21.74)	5 (50.00)	6 (35.29)	6 (66.67)	9 (40.91)	4 (33.33)	23 (30.26)	21 (46.67)
Total	14 (100.00)	14 (100.00)	23 (100.00)	10 (100.00)	17 (100.00)	9 (100.00)	22 (100.00)	12 (100.00)	76 (100.00)	45 (100.00)

Note: Figures in brackets represent % age.

Table—4.15: Occupation of female spouses among sample households

Occupation	*Brahman*	*Chasa*	*Bauri*	*Santal*	*Total*
(1)	*(2)*	*(3)*	*(4)*	*(5)*	*(6)*
Housekeeping	49 (98.00)	46 (92.00)	5 (10.00)	7 (14.00)	107 (53.50)
Petty business	–	3 (6.00)	2 (4.00)	2 (4.00)	7 (3.5)
Service	1 (2.00)	–	–	–	1 (0.5)
Wage-earning	–	1 (2.00)	43 (86.00)	41 (82.00)	85 (42.5)
Total	50 (100.00)	50 (100.00)	50 (100.00)	50 (100.00)	200 (100.00)

Note: Figures in brackets represent % age.

Table—4.16: Management of money earned by employed/wage-earning female spouses

	Brahman (N = 1)	*Chasa* (N = 4)	*Bauri* (N = 45)	*Santal* (N = 43)	*Total* (N = 93)
(1)	(2)	(3)	(4)	(5)	(6)
Whole amount is given to the male spouses	–	4 (100.00)	25 (55.50)	26 (60.47)	55 (59.14)
A major part is given to the male spouses and a minor part is kept with self	1 (100.00)	–	–	–	1 (1.08)
Whole amount is kept with self	–	–	20 (44.44)	17 (39.53)	37 (39.78)

Note: Figures in brackets represent % age.

Table—4.17: Consequences if the employed/wage-earning female spouses do not give the money earned by them to their male spouses

Consequences	*Brahman* (N = 1)	*Chasa* (N = 4)	*Bauri* (N = 45)	*Santal* (N = 43)	*Total* (N = 93)
(1)	(2)	(3)	(4)	(5)	(6)
Husband takes by force	1 (100.00)	1 (25.00)	38 (84.44)	39	78 (83.87)
Threatens to divorce	–	–	17 (37.78)	–	17 (18.28)
Nothing	–	3 (75.00)	–	4 (9.30)	7 (7.53)

Note: Figures in brackets represent % age.

5

Women and Legislative Measures

Traditionally, in India, men and women did not enjoy equal social status because of various factors associated with many socio-cultural and religious norms and regulations made by the ancient law-givers. Ancient law-makers, like Yagyavalkya and Manu have weighted men as superior to that of women and hence placed them on the higher side and considered women as commodities or even as servants of men. This has caused women as subservient to men and hence, they suffer from various disabilities. As a result, compared to men, women have remained very backward on social, economic, educational, political and religious fronts. But, after independence, many social activities and administrative action-planners in India thought that the country would not grow keeping pace with the progress of the developed countries unless women of this country are socially and legally equated with men. Serious attempts were made to rootout the traditional inequalities and social prejudices prevailing against women. With the active cooperation and will of the political executives, various legal provisions were made in the Indian Constitution, and progressive legislations were enacted. Thus, laws came into operation. The Constitution also empowered States (Act, 38) to "adopt measures of positive discrimination in favour of women for neturalising the cumulative socio-economic, educational and political disadvantages faced by them" (G.O.I., 1998: 1) and hence to bring them into the mainstream at par with men.

The Constitution of India also provides all those rights to women which are given to men (Gangrade, 1978: 4-23 in Ahuja, 1992: 7). The fundamental rights proclaimed in various Articles (14 and 15) of the Constitution have ensured equality to all irrespective of any sex before law and ensure equal protection; prohibit discrimination against any citizen on the ground of religion, race, caste, sex or place of birth. Other important Articles that are more or less women specific include Art. 16, Art. 39, Art. 40, Art. 41, Art. 42, Art. 43, Art. 44, Art 45, Art. 47, Art. 325, Art. 526 etc. (cf. Constitution of India; Sachchidanada, 1984: 4-5, and Ahuja, 1992: 7-8). These Articles are related to right to freedom of speech, expression, residence, occupation, public assistance, exploitation, religion, property, education, election on the basis of adult franchise, access to nutrition and public health care services etc. Apart from these constitutional provisions, various social, economic and political legislative measures have also been formulated and enacted at various points of time in order to fulfil the constitutional commitments especially in relation to upliftment of the girl children and the women of our country. Some of such legislations are: the Child Marriage Restraint Act, 1929; the Special Marriage Act, 1954; the Hindu Marriage Act, 1955; the Special Marriage Act, 1955; the Hindu Adoption and Maintenance Act, 1956; the Hindu Succession Act, 1956; the Dowry Prohibition Act, 1961; the Maternity Benefit Act, 1961; the Special Marriage Act, 1984; the Medical Termination of Pregnancy Act, 1971; the Equal Remuneration Act, 1978; the Immoral Traffic (Prevention) Act, 1986; the Indecent Representation of Women (Prohibition) Act, 1986; and the Commission of *Sati* (Prevention) Act, 1987. These legislations can broadly be categorised into two sectors such as, (A) legislations on social sector and (B) legislations on economic sector.

A. Legislations on Social Sector

(a) The Hindu Marriage Act, 1955 (Amended in 1987)

(i) *Minimum Age:* This Act prescribes 18 years for a girl and 21 years for a boy as their minimum ages for getting married provided neither has a spouse at the time of marriage.

(ii) *Right of Women on Selection of Life:* Under this Act, a girl of 18 years enjoys the legal right to select her own life partner outside her own caste, sub-caste, community or even religion. But, if such a marriage tie is sought by a girl, legally it must be registered under the court of the competent authority (Marriage Officer) and such a marriage may not entail any customary or religious ceremonies.

(iii) *Right of Wife to Divorce:* The Special Marriage Act, 1954 and the Hindu Marriage Act, 1955 permit only monogamy and treat bigamy as an offence. In no case these Acts permit any person to marry more than one spouse at a point of time. These provide legal rights to a female spouse to divorce her husband, if the latter takes a second wife through proper solemnization by way of performing rituals and ceremonies as per the prevailing social customs and religious codes of conduct. This is also applicable to a man to divorce his wife on the same ground, i.e. if his wife marries a second husband as per the prevailing ceremonial customs.

Apart from this, both the said Acts entitle either spouse for legal separation or divorce on the following grounds:

— Adultery, i.e. voluntary sexual intercourse between a married person and a person (married or not) other than his/her spouse;

— Cruelty in behaviour;

— Conversion to another religion without the consent or will of the other spouse;

— Imprisonment for illegal acts;

— Mental illness or unsoundness of mind for a period of 3 years continuously;

— Suffering from major communicable diseases, like leprosy or venereal diseases for 3 consecutive years;

— Renunciation;

- — Desertion for two consecutive years;
- — One spouse being not heard of living status of the other spouse for a minimum period of 7 years or more;
- — Developing impotency, i.e. lacking of ability to procreate children;
- — Obtaining of consent of someone to marry by applying of physical or any other force or marrying someone by providing false information;
- — Detection of being pregnant of the female spouse by someone other than the husband;
- — Failure to resume co-habitation with a decree for restitution of conjugal rights;
- — After mutual consent of either party showing that the spouses have been staying separately since last one year without having any conjugation and they are unable to be friendly again after an estrangement.

(b) Maintenance and Custody of Children

According to the Hindu Adoption and Maintenance Act, 1956, the wife and the legitimate children are entitled to be maintained by her husband. So, during the period of judicial proceedings on a separation case, legally the husband is supposed to financially assist his wife (and also his children left with the wife) even if during that period they stay separately and do not lead conjugal life as husband and wife. The gross sum to be given by the husband is fixed up by the Court of Law depending upon the financial condition of either parties. Even after divorce, the female spouse is expected to get maintenance charges from her husband. But she gets this benefit only until she remains moral. Once she becomes immoral or gets married to some other person means, she is to be debarred from this benefit.

As per the Hindu Minority and Guardianship Act-1956, when the wife and husband are legally separated or are divorced from each other, generally the children below 5 years of age remain under the custody of their mother and the father does enjoy and legal right to be the custodian of such children. However, the father remains as the natural guardian of those children. He may legally enforce his right on them after such children complete 5 years of age.

(c) Restitution of Conjugal Rights

A woman may leave her husband's home because of nagging and illtreatment by her in-laws, cruelty or drunkard nature of her husband, dowry torture etc. After some days or years her husband may persuade her to come back and reconcile but his wife may not accept the proposal. In that case he may ask for the help of the Court of Law. In such a case "when the court grants a husband's request for his wife's company and wife refuses to go with her husband, the court cannot penalise her for disobeying the decree of restitution of conjugal rights or imprison her or attack her property" (Ahuja, 1992: 17-18). It may also happen that after some days or years, the wife likes to come back but the husband may refuse to take her back and in that case she may also file a case against her husband. But in this case, the husband is bound to obey the order of the court otherwise "his property may be attack according to civil procedure code. The consequence of the wife not following the decree is that after one year of separation, either party would be entitled to divorce the other" (ibid: p. 18).

(d) The Child Marriage Restraint Act, 1929

This Act prescribes 18 years for a boy and 14 years for a girl as the minimum ages for marriages. The age of the girl was later on amended to 15 years and hence the Act prohibits child marriage, i.e. marriage of an immatured girl was has not attained puberty. This was normally prevalent among the caste Hindus as per their the-then religious code of conducts and social mores and customs. The Act prescribes various punishments for the deviants and the close associates. However, the Hindu Marriage Act, 1955 amended in 1978 raised the minimum age of the girl to 18 years and that of the boy to 21 years for being eligible to get married.

(e) *Dowry Prohibition*

In the past, Hindus practiced a general form of marriage in which the parents of a girl gave a handful amount of gifts to their daughters in the form of valuable ornaments, households assets, ration, cash or even landed properties with or without fruitbearing trees etc. This was known as *Stridhan* or *Kanyadhan* on which the bride had absolute ownership right. She was spending those in any form she was thinking appropriate. During that period the amount of *stridhan* was not considered as a criterion for finalising marriage of a boy at some particular family rather the caste, economic and social positions, beauty and nature of the bride, compatibility of horoscope etc., were considered as important criteria for this. But during the later part of the British regime in India, this tradition gradually lost its significance since dowry system came into force because of the growth of population and thereby unemployment. It caused unavailability of suitable grooms in the marriage market, as a result rich parents of brides tried to pick up the better grooms by providing much dowry and subsequently it became commercialised. The people considered dowry as one of the main considerations for fixing up a marriage. The rich could do like this but the middle class people faced a lot of problem for arranging considerable amount of dowry in order to match their daughters with suitable employed and educated grooms. Once the amount of dowry is fixed before a marriage means, the parents of the bride are to give the whole amount otherwise, the in-laws and the husband torture or harass the bride in various forms, and thus, achieving the real goals of marriage get disturbed (cf. Sachchidananda, 1984: 39-41). In order to rootout this social evil, in 1961, Dowry Prohibition Act was enacted that prohibits giving or agreeing to give dowry in any form either at the time of marriage or after this by one party and taking it by the other party. It is considered as an offence and punishable under the law.

(f) *Widow Remarriage and Prevention of Sati*

Hindu religion does not permit a widow to remarry rather as per the codes of conduct of this religion, a wife must remain chasteful and loyal to her husband and after the death of her husband, she must sacrifice herself in the pyre of her husband in order to justify her truthfulness towards him. By doing this, it was thought that both of them were getting *Mukti* or mundane salvation. But in 1964, a special Act relating to marriage was passed that permits the widows or divorcees to remarry according to their own choices and in that case if the widow has some male or female issues, the guardianship of such children would remain in the hands of the male relatives of the deceased husband. Subsequently, in 1987 *Sati* Prevention Act was also commissioned. According to this Act, no widow could sacrifice herself as *Sati* at the funeral pyre of her deceased husband. It is considered as a crime and hence the culprits are punishable under law.

(g) Adoption of Children

In patrilineal Caste Hindu societies, the role of a male child is very important as a socio-religious as well as economic necessity and old-age security. He is also entitled to inherit ancestral property and to maintain this and also for discharging many ritualistic duties, like offering *mukhagni* to his dead parent and also performing annual *sradha* ceremonies in favour of his forefathers extending to at least 7 generations. In this regard, the Hindu Adoption and Maintenance Act that was passed in 1956 permits an issueless parent to adopt a son or a daughter depending upon its own choice. Even, this Act also permits an unmarried woman or a widow or a divorcee to adopt a child of its own choice. A married woman can also adopt an unmarried child below the age of 15 years if her husband has become mad or changed his religion and does not produce any child.

(h) Abortion of Unwanted Child

An important legislation relating to abortion of unwanted children was passed in 1971 which came into force in 1972. This legislation is known as the Medical Termination of Pregnancy (MTP) Act-1971. The salient features of this Act are as follows:

(i) A woman has the right to terminate her pregnancy through artificial methods within 12 weeks by a

registered doctor but if the pregnancy has exceeded 12 weeks but not 20 weeks she can do so with the help of at least two such doctors only if the doctor/s is/are of the opinion that the concerned pregnancy would cause severe mental or physical health deterioration of the mother or there is any life risk for the mother of the child.

(ii) She can terminate the pregnancy if it has happened because of rape or unwanted intercourse with a person.

(iii) A married pregnant woman is also permitted to medically terminated her pregnancy if it has occurred because of failure of any family planning method adopted by her or her husband in order to limit the family size or the birth of the concerned child would cause any injury to the mental health of the pregnant lady.

(iv) The termination of any pregnancy can only be done at government hospitals or at places approved by the government.

(i) Suppression and Prohibition of Immortal Trafficking in Women and Girls

In some societies, women and girls are compelled to practice prostitution either because of their poor economic condition or because of their tradition or for some other reasons. In 1956, an Act called 'The Suppression of Immoral Traffic in Women and Girls was passed and thereafter the Immoral Traffic (Prevention) Act, 1986 was passed. These Act Prohibit immoral trafficking in women and girls and the persons who are either directly or indirectly involved in the matter are considered as culprits and are punished under law.

(j) Prohibition of Indecent Representation of Women and Girls

Nowadays, many advertising companies are giving much importance to launch or market the commercial products with the indecently picturised presentation of women and girls in order to attract the customers, particularly men. This, definitely hampers the social image of women. So, in order to protect this interest of them, the Indecent Representation of Women (Prohibition) Act was passed in 1986 that prohibits indecent representation of women through advertisement in books, magazines, newspapers, or in any other such materials.

(B) Legislations on Economic Sectors

Various economic interests of Indian caste Hindu women have been protected through a number of legislative measures. These are related to their rights on inheritance of property (paternal, maternal, affinal and also those earned by themselves or any other), equal wage for equal work, maternity benefits, job securities etc.

(i) Inheritance of Property

In traditional patriarchal caste Hindu societies where lineage is traced in the male line, women lack any right to inherit any paternal (excepting *Shtridhan*) or affinal properties basing on the thoughts of *Dayabhag* and *Mitakshyar* schools. But in order to remove this disparity, a legislation called Hindu Succession Act was passed in 1956, which provides equal rights of succession to both the male and females persons of a family and has condemned the traditional systems of inheritance of property under the above two schools of thought those discriminate the women.

This Act has removed the distinction between *Shtridhan* and *non-shtridhan* as was prevailing during the past and categorised the property of a Hindu women into 3 groups as follows:

(i) Property which she inherits from her husband or father-in-law, (ii) Property which she inherits from her parents, (iii) Property other than those falling under the above two categories (Ahuja, 1992: 25).

The most important aspect of this Act is that "the widow (if there are more widows than one, they together), the mother, sons and daughters of the deceased person get one share each. If any son has expired, his widow, sons and daughters, if any, divide the share which he would have got if he was alive, each getting one share. In any daughter has expired, her sons and daughters (but not the husband) divide equally the share which their mother, if alive, would have got" (ibid, p. 24).

The above Act also signifies that "any property possessed by a female Hindu, whether acquired before or after the commencement of the Act, shall be held by her on full ownership thereof and not as a limited owner" (Subramanyam, 1991: 52).

(ii) Equal Wage for Equal Work

Occupation of a person is generally determined according to sex depending upon the sexual division of labour. Generally women are engaged in such works that are less laborious and also involve less social prestige. However, many times, both men and women are also engaged or employed in similar types of work but women are paid less wage or remuneration than their male co-workers even if the output of the former workers is more than the latter. In order to eradicate this social disparity, the Equal Remuneration Act, 1976 prescribes equal wage for equal work and empowered women workers to seek the help of the court of law if they are discriminated against in this regard.

(iii) Maternity Benefit and the Women Workers

Women are bio-physically designed to carry foetus and give birth to children which the men cannot do. During pregnancy, a woman needs much care and rest with a view to give birth to a healthy and sound child. If she works hard, and physically as well as mentally remains unhealthy, its repercussion is reflected on the foetus. So, in order to provide them social security, a legislative measure relating to maternity benefit was enacted in 1961 that provides various maternity benefits to an expectant mother. The benefits include leave before and after the birth of the child with full pay and job security during that period, medical benefits and other such benefits, like payment of maternity benefit in case of death of a woman, leave for miscarriage, leave for illness arising out of pregnancy; delivery; premature birth of the child or miscarriage, nursing breaks in daily work until the child attains 15 months of age etc. (cf. ibid, pp. 124-35).

(iv) Personality, Women and Job Security

The labour laws specify that in no case a women be dismissed from her job charging her with misconduct. However, she may be suspended but she is entitled to get subsistence allowance during the period of judicial proceedings (Ahuja, 1992: 26-27).

Apart from the above provisions for the welfare of women, there are some other benefits available for the women working in industrial establishments.

The Factory Act, 1948 and also the Contract Labour (Regulation and Abolition) Central Rules, 1971 specify various provisions on behalf of the women workers. The important provisions include:

- *(i)* Specific latrine and urinal facilities (at least one for each of 25 female workers);
- *(ii)* Creche facility during office hours with all amenities, like sufficient staff to look after the children, first-aid box, equipments, like cradles or cots, beds or mattresses, cotton sheets, rubber sheets, blankets, pillows with cover etc.
- *(iii)* Rest rooms;
- *(iv)* Canteen facility within the premises of such establishments where they work;
- *(v)* Working hours limiting to maximum 9 hours a day and no employment of these workers in night shifts, i.e. from 10 pm to 5 am etc. (Subramanyam, 1991: pp. 4-11 and Ahuja, 1992: 26-27).

6

Level of Awareness on Protective Measures and the Need of Social Intervention

In the preceding chapter, we have vividly discussed the protective measures meant for the girl children and the women of our country. In this chapter, an attempt has been made to assess the awareness level of the sample population on some of such measures; viz, age at marriage, selection of mate and right to divorce, widow re-marriage and adoption of child, dowry prohibition, medical termination of pregnancy, inheritance and disposal of property and equal wage opportunity for equal work done by any person.

Maternity and Age at Marriage

'Age' is an important factor in one's life since it determines the social and physical status of a person. It also plays a significant role in one's personal career-building. However, the role of 'age' is very closely related with the bio-physiological condition of a person, be it a man or a woman. So, at what age, a girl or a boy should get married be very thoughtfully judged, otherwise the life course of the concerned persons is shattered. In cases where proper decision relating to 'age at marriage' of a person, particularly of a girl, is not judiciously taken, after marriage, her physical and mental health severely deteriorates that might lead her to death.

In our country, we had a strange practice of child marriage prevalent in many societies for a very long period of time. By this tradition, immatured girls had to marry immatured boys or young men. But marital conjugation was preferably allowed only after the maturity of the bride, since attaining of maturity was widely considered as the most important factor or often the sole criteria for allowing her to become a mother. Even now, this idea still persists among many people of traditional societies, as a result of which parents becomes very embarrassed when their daughters attain puberty. They feel such daughters as social as well as economic burden on them and search for suitable grooms for them even though medically it has been proved that simply attaining maturity does not physically permit a girl to bear a child in her womb or become a mother.

The available census data also substantiate the traditional practice as in the early past of the last century, i.e. during the decade of 1901-11, the average age at marriage of girls was only "13.3 years", (Ahuja, 1992: 51). However, in the subsequent period of time, it increased to 15.4 years in 1951, 16.1 years in 1961, and 17.1 year in 1971. In 1976, the Child Marriage Restraint (Amendment) Act came into force by which the minimum age for marriage of girls was fixed at 18 years of age but in the year 1981, the mean age at marriage for girls was found to be below (17.9 years) this specified age. And how, it came to 19.5 years in 1992 and 19.6 years in 1993. However, these figures certainly indicate that there is no much difference between the rate of growth of mean age at marriage of females occurred during these two periods, vis 1901 to 1971 and after legal introduction of Child Marriage Restraint Act in 1971. It is mainly because of the fact that most of the Indian people reside in rural areas and as such they have remained unaware of the Act made on this respect and there is a sustained interest among the men to marry younger girls. What is surprising is that many people based in urban areas or urban fringes are also not aware of the fact since the initiatives taken by the government in order to provide awareness generation among the public on the legislative matters is very poor and hence not appreciable.

The data pertaining to the present study also show the same thing as of the total of 200 men and 200 women only 19.50 per cent men as against merely 10.5 per cent of women are aware of the Act, i.e. minimum age for marriage of a girl prescribed by the government. However, the awareness of Bauri and Santal people on this Act is almost nil. It is only the Brahman community, of which 54 per cent men as against 34 per cent of women are aware of the fact. This might be because of their higher educational status and superior cultural background. The awareness level of the Chasa people is little better than the Bauris and Santals but much lower to that of the Brahmans (Table 6.1).

So far as the knowledge on the minimum age prescribed for men to get married is concerned, a total number of 30 men and women, each irrespective of any community, is found to have knowledge about this. They account for 15 per cent of the total population interviewed. The rest people do not possess any knowledge on this subject.

Selection of Mate and Right to Divorce

Indian people are very tradition-bound and have fear of the displeasure of the supernatural forces to a large extent. So they do not like to deviate from the cultural set practices prevailing since generations. As for instance, the orthodox Indian people have deep faith in the doctrine of their own caste. As such, they do not allow their children to go in for marriages which go against the set practices and interests of their caste, sub-caste, community or religion. More particularly, inter-caste, inter-community or inter-religion marriages are not accepted by them. In any person goes against the ethics of its caste or religion by deviating from the accepted norms and regulations, it may be astracised from the family and hence may also be deprived of the ancestral property. However, the Hindu Marriage Act, 1956, amended in 1978, empowers the Hindus, particularly the women to select their own life partner outside their caste, sub-caste, community or even religion. But the knowledge of the public on this issue is very poor.

In the present study, only a total number of 68 married men irrespective of any caste, accounting for 34 per cent of the total sample as against 90 married female spouses or 45 per cent say that women should have the right to select their life partners (Table 6.3) but certainly not outside of their caste, sub-caste, community or religion (Table 6.4). The rest persons say that being women they should not have this right rather they should be satisfied with the decision of their parents, preferably fathers, as regards selection of their life partners. However, as many as 143 or 71.50 per cent men as against 180 or 90 per cent women do not know that as per the Hindu Marriage Act, 1956, girls aged 18 years old have right to select their own life-partners outside their caste, sub-caste, community or even religion (Table 6.5).

As discussed in the previous chapter, the Hindu Marriage Act-1955 prohibits bigamy. So, if the husband marries a second wife with all the formal socio-religious rituals, the wife may divorce her husband. She is also empowered to divorce her husband for the same reasons her husband would divorce her as per the legal provisions. But only 18 per cent of males as against 7.50 per cent of females of the total have knowledge about this provisions. However, maximum percentage of Brahman male (36.00) and female (14.00) are found to be aware of the Act as compared to others (Table 6.7). Further the same table also indicates that the awareness of the females of all the caste communities is much lower the awareness level of their male counterparts.

Widow Remarriage and Adoption of Children

Remaining as a widow after the death of husband is a very important social attitude in Hindu religion. As such, this religion does not permit a widow to remarry. However, among the folk or tribal communities, widow remarriage is a very common phenomenon. Because more often they consider wives as economic assets rather than simply biological social entities of the family. As a result they do not like to spoil the youth of young widows who could be utilised for bread earning as well as for satisfying the emotional and other goals of marriage. So, almost all the male and female respondents of the Santal community favour the idea of widow remarriage and consider that there is no harm if one goes against the practice. However, there are only 16 per cent of Brahman males as against 20 per cent of Chasa and 22 per cent of Bauri males who maintain that a widow should get remarried. Women who also favour the system, account for 24 per cent in case of the Brahman community, 22 per cent in case of the Chasa community and 26 per cent in case of the Bauri community. Thus, among all the communities, there are more female than male who say that the widows should remarry and there is nothing negative in it. The rest, do not like the idea rather they profess that as per the tradition, a widow must remain as widow until her last breath by respecting her dead husband and family tradition (Table 6.8). However, there are very few persons who are aware of the legal provision pertaining to widow remarriage. There are only 39 males accounting for 19.5 per cent of the total 200 respondents who know that as per the legal provision a widow can remarry. The respective percentage for the females is only 11.50. However, there is none among the Santals who know about this social reform. The case of the Bauri people is also more or less the same. There are only Brahman and Chasa communities, of which few male and female persons are found to have knowledge on the said legal provision. However, there are more men (48.00%) and women (34.00%) in the Brahman community as against 45 per cent of Chasa men and 12 per cent of women who are found to have knowledge on this social reform.

In order to protect some vital life-supporting interests of Indian women, government has also made a legal provision by which a widow, an unmarried woman or a divorcee can adopt a child of her own choice. But this reform is not widely accepted and hence not popular among the rural as well as urban population. The present findings indicate that not a single male or female person of any community is in favour of the idea. They say that an unmarried girl should not adopt a child (Table 6.10). According to them if a girl remains unmarried for any reason, she must be very polite and well courteous with her brothers and sisters-in-law so that she would lead a peaceful and problem-free life. But if she demands a share out of the paternal property or adopts a child, there may be confrontation between herself and other family members, particularly with the brothers and their wives. In such a case her life course would be very difficult. However, there are 11 per cent males as against 21 per cent of females who say that a widow should adopt a child and the rest oppose this idea (Table 6.11). Those who are against this idea say that if a widow adopts a child, a similar situation as mentioned above would also arise. But in this case, the elder or younger brothers of the deceased (husband) of the widow would go against her. They would do so with a hope that they would get her property after she dies. As a result, the widow must adjust with the situation by asking for maintenance from the brothers of her deceased husband but she cannot elicit their sympathy by adopting a child. However, she should adopt one of the children of any brother of her deceased husband if she so desires. But in no case adoption of an outside child is appreciated by such brothers. If it is done so, the widow would have to struggle hard and hence, she would not lead a peaceful life. However, so far as the legal provisions on this aspect is concerned there is none in any of the communities, viz Brahman, Chasa, Bauri or Santal, who is found to have knowledge about the fact that an unmarried girl can adopt a child (Table 6.12). But there are few persons who are aware that legality the widows are entitled to adopt children (Table 6.13).

Dowry Prohibition and its Effects

Giving or taking dowry in any form is punishable under the law since this has been banned under the Dowry Prohibition Act, 1961. But quite a good number of people, i.e. 29.33 per cent of males as against 34.67 per cent of females say that a person should give dowry on the marriage of her daughter so that she would lead a better life. But the rest 70.67 per cent of men and 65.33 per cent of women are against this system, since it has various negative impact on the family members of both the parties and also on the society as a whole. However, compared to the Bauri and Chasa people, there are more percentage of Brahman men (48.00%) and women (74.00%) who favour the system since they consider it as a religious issue required for the welfare of the married daughters (Table 6.14). However, compared to other legislations made for the welfare of women quite a good number of men and women are aware about the legal prohibition of dowry since various media are very seriously advertising on this issue. Data presented in Table 6.15 show that irrespective of any community, there are as high as 34.67 per cent of men as against 21.33 per cent of women who are aware about the legal prohibition of dowry. But as in other legislative matters, more Brahman men (60.00%) and women (36.00%) are there who have knowledge about this social reform. The Chasa men and women who are aware of this fact account for 32 and 20 per cent respectively. The corresponding figures for Bauri men and women are merely 12 and 8 per cent respectively.

Medical Termination of Pregnancy and the Girl Child

In India, women are considered as if they are born only to give birth to children. Even in many rural communities the social status of a woman who gives birth to a number of children is more than those who have no child. Hence, a mother of a number of children feels very proud and often cites herself as a good example for others. So a mother does not like to spoil the time by keeping long space between children rather than goes on procreating children one after another without any gap between progenies during her potential maternity period. Many times she is also compelled to procreate children as many as she can. This, of course deteriorates the health status of the mother as well as that of the children born to her. But certainly a mother who has more number of girl children is not respected in the family or in the society. She is humiliated and even tortured in various ways, as if she is responsible for that. However, because of modernization of medical technology, nowadays the sex of the foetus is easily being identified and women are being pressurised by their husbands or family members to terminate the female foetus. But women have been legally empowered to protect themselves as well as the female foetus. Termination of pregnancy is only possible if the concerned pregnancy would cause physical or mental deterioration of the mother or that of the child and also for some other reasons, mentioned in the previous chapter. But many people are still unaware of this legal provision. The present study shows that out of the total population, there are only 24 or 12 per cent of women as against 37 or 18.5% of men who have knowledge about medical termination of pregnancy and the rest people are unaware about this matter. However, there is not a single man or woman, either in Bauri community or in Santal community, who is aware of this but there are 38 per cent of Brahman men as against 40 per cent of women who know that termination of pregnancy is illegal. The corresponding figures for Chasa men and women are found to be 36 per cent and 8 per cent respectively.

Provisions of Equal Wage for Equal Work

The provision of equal wage for equal work is a very positive look of the government towards the women workers. But most of the people have remained unaware of this provision since there has been no significant initiative taken by the government to popularise the provision amongst the general mass, particularly, among the rural poors. As a result they have remained ignorant of it and hence, fall prey to the brokers, petty contractors or the employers. As per the present study it comes to the fore that there are only 8 or 16 per cent of Brahman men as against only 6 or 12 per cent of Chasa men together accounting for 14 or 7 per cent of the total sample of 200 of all the communities who are aware of this legal provision but there is not a single woman in any community who is found to be aware of this social reform and legal provision (Table 6.17).

So far as the minimum wage per day for the unskilled wage earners is concerned, government of Orissa had fixed up it at Rs. 11 in 90's. It was raised to Rs. 25 during the Chief Ministership of late Biju Pattanaik and thereafter it was further increased to Rs. 30. Presently, this amount has been fixed up at Rs. 40 (The Samaj, Apl. 29th, 1999). But the awareness level of the public on the present minimum wage fixed for an unskilled labourer is very poor. A total number of 39 or 19.5 per cent of men as against only 9 or 4.5 per cent of women of the total sample are there who possess knowledge on this matter, but there is not a single man or woman in the Bauri community who is found to have knowledge on this legislation. However, more or less the same percentage of Brahman and Chasa men (36%) and women (8%) know about the minimum wage fixed by the government. However, there are only 2 Santal men who are also aware of this matter (Table 6.18).

Inheritance of Paternal Property

As per the legal provision mentioned earlier, girl children have been privileged to get an equal share of paternal property along with the boy children. In this regard they cannot be discriminated in any manner against boy children. But only 90 per cent of men as against nearly 20 per cent of women are aware of this. However, compared to Bauri and Santal communities, there are more men and women among the Brahman and Chasa communities who are found to have knowledge about this matter (Table 6.19). However, there are 32 or 16 per cent of women as against 19 or 9.5 per cent of men irrespective of any community who are of the opinion that the wife should not have the right to inherit an equal share of the paternal property. But the rest do not agree with them. Those who say that women should not have any right to get an equal share of paternal property, argue that as per the tradition, women are economically dependent on their spouses. Secondly they are to leave their paternal home after their marriage and permanently stay with their affines. Hence, there is no need for a woman to get a share of property which her parents inherit. If they get a share, it would reduce the economic condition of sons who are traditionally required to inherit and look after the ancestral properties and old parents. However, even if women are legally entitled to have an equal share of paternal property, in reality they should not claim. If any woman exercises this right, her social relationship with her brothers is immediately cut off and she remains socially isolated, particularly from the family of her brothers and hence, the social relationship between the children and brothers and sisters gets strained. Therefore, married daughters, sisters and father's sisters do not claim a share of their paternal properties even if legally they are entitled to get their share.

Table—6.1: Knowledge of minimum age prescribed for marriage of a female

Variables	*Brahman*		*Chasa*		*Bauri*		*Santal*		*Total*	
	M	*F*	*M*	*F*	*M*	*F*	*M*	*F*	*M*	*F*
(1)	*(2)*	*(3)*	*(4)*	*(5)*	*(6)*	*(7)*	*(8)*	*(9)*	*(10)*	*(11)*
Have	27 (54.00)	17 (34.00)	8 (16.00)	3 (6.00)	1 (2.00)	–	3 (6.00)	1 (2.00)	39 (19.50)	21 (10.5)
Do not have	23 (46.00)	33 (66.00)	42 (84.00)	47 (94.00)	49 (98.00)	50 (100.00)	47 (94.00)	49 (98.00)	161 (80.5)	179 (89.50)
Total	50 (100.00)	50 (100.00)	50 (100.00)	50 (100.00)	50 (100.00)	50 (100.00)	50 (100.00)	50 (100.00)	200 (100.00)	200 (100.00)

Note: *(i)* 'M' and 'F' stand for male spouse and female spouse respectively.

(ii) Figures in brackets represent % age.

Table—6.2: Knowledge on minimum age prescribed for marriage of a male

Variables	*Brahman*		*Chasa*		*Bauri*		*Santal*		*Total*	
	M	*F*	*M*	*F*	*M*	*F*	*M*	*F*	*M*	*F*
(1)	*(2)*	*(3)*	*(4)*	*(5)*	*(6)*	*(7)*	*(8)*	*(9)*	*(10)*	*(11)*
Have	23 (46.00)	19 (38.00)	7 (14.00)	3 (6.00)	–	–	4 (8.00)	–	30 (15.00)	30 (15.00)
Do not have	27 (54.00)	31 (62.00)	43 (86.00)	47 (94.00)	50 (100.00)	50 (100.00)	46 (92.00)	50 (100.00)	170 (85.00)	170 (85.00)
Total	50 (100.00)	50 (100.00)	50 (100.00)	50 (100.00)	50 (100.00)	50 (100.00)	50 (100.00)	50 (100.00)	200 (100.00)	200 (100.00)

Note: As per Table—6.1.

Table—6.3: Whether a girl should have the right to choose her life partner within her caste, sub-caste community or religion?

Answers	*Brahman*		*Chasa*		*Bauri*		*Santal*		*Total*	
	M	*F*	*M*	*F*	*M*	*F*	*M*	*F*	*M*	*F*
(1)	*(2)*	*(3)*	*(4)*	*(5)*	*(6)*	*(7)*	*(8)*	*(9)*	*(10)*	*(11)*
Yes	8 (16.00)	11 (22.00)	10 (20.00)	14 (28.00)	18 (36.00)	18 (36.00)	32 (64.00)	37 (74.00)	68 (34.00)	90 (45.00)
No	42 (84.00)	39 (78.00)	40 (80.00)	36 (72.00)	32 (64.00)	32 (64.00)	18 (36.00)	13 (26.00)	132 (66.00)	110 (55.00)
Total	50 (100.00)	50 (100.00)	50 (100.00)	50 (100.00)	50 (100.00)	50 (100.00)	50 (100.00)	50 (100.00)	200 (100.00)	200 (100.00)

Note: As per Table—6.1.

Table—6.4: Whether the girl should have the right to choose her life partner outside her caste, sub-caste community or religion?

Answers	*Brahman*		*Chasa*		*Bauri*		*Santal*		*Total*	
	M	*F*	*M*	*F*	*M*	*F*	*M*	*F*	*M*	*F*
(1)	*(2)*	*(3)*	*(4)*	*(5)*	*(6)*	*(7)*	*(8)*	*(9)*	*(10)*	*(11)*
Yes	–	–	–	–	–	–	–	–	–	–
No	50 (100.00)	50 (100.00)	50 (100.00)	50 (100.00)	50 (100.00)	50 (100.00)	50 (100.00)	50 (100.00)	200 (100.00)	200 (100.00)
Total	50 (100.00)	50 (100.00)	50 (100.00)	50 (100.00)	50 (100.00)	50 (100.00)	50 (100.00)	50 (100.00)	200 (100.00)	200 (100.00)

Note: As per Table—6.1.

Table—6.5: Knowledge of the right of the females to choose their life partners outside caste, sub-caste, community or religion

Variables	*Brahman*		*Chasa*		*Bauri*		*Santal*		*Total*	
	M	*F*	*M*	*F*	*M*	*F*	*M*	*F*	*M*	*F*
(1)	*(2)*	*(3)*	*(4)*	*(5)*	*(6)*	*(7)*	*(8)*	*(9)*	*(10)*	*(11)*
Have	18 (36.00)	10 (20.00)	13 (26.00)	7 (14.00)	6 (12.00)	3 (6.00)	– –	– –	37 (18.50)	20 (10.00)
Do not have	32 (64.00)	40 (80.00)	37 (74.00)	43 (86.00)	44 (88.00)	47 (94.00)	50 (100.00)	50 (100.00)	143 (71.50)	180 (90.00)
Total	50 (100.00)	50 (100.00)	50 (100.00)	50 (100.00)	50 (100.00)	50 (100.00)	50 (100.00)	50 (100.00)	200 (100.00)	200 (100.00)

Note: As per Table—6.1.

Table—6.6: Do you think that the wife should have the right to divorce her husband for the same reasons a husband divorces his wife?

Answers	*Brahmans*		*Chasa*		*Bauri*		*Santal*		*Total*	
	M	*F*	*M*	*F*	*M*	*F*	*M*	*F*	*M*	*F*
(1)	*(2)*	*(3)*	*(4)*	*(5)*	*(6)*	*(7)*	*(8)*	*(9)*	*(10)*	*(11)*
Yes	1 (2.00)	4 (8.00)	9 (18.00)	9 (18.00)	13 (26.00)	7 (14.00)	18 (36.00)	31 (62.00)	41 (20.50)	51 (25.50)
No	49 (98.00)	46 (92.00)	41 (82.00)	41 (82.00)	37 (74.00)	43 (86.00)	32 (64.00)	19 (38.00)	159 (79.50)	149 (74.50)
Total	50 (100.00)	50 (100.00)	50 (100.00)	50 (100.00)	50 (100.00)	50 (100.00)	50 (100.00)	50 (100.00)	200 (100.00)	200 (100.00)

Note: As per Table—6.1.

Table—6.7: Knowledge of the right of woman to divorce her husband for the same reasons a husband divorces his wife

Variables	*Brahman*		*Chasa*		*Bauri*		*Santal*		*Total*	
	M	*F*	*M*	*F*	*M*	*F*	*M*	*F*	*M*	*F*
(1)	*(2)*	*(3)*	*(4)*	*(5)*	*(6)*	*(7)*	*(8)*	*(9)*	*(10)*	*(11)*
Have	18 (36.00)	7 (14.00)	6 (12.00)	3 (6.00)	8 (16.00)	2 (4.00)	4 (8.00)	3 (6.00)	36 (18.00)	15 (7.50)
Do not have	32 (64.00)	43 (86.00)	44 (88.00)	47 (94.00)	42 (84.00)	48 (96.00)	46 (92.00)	47 (94.00)	164 (82.00)	185 (92.50)
Total	50 (100.00)	50 (100.00)	50 (100.00)	50 (100.00)	50 (100.00)	50 (100.00)	50 (100.00)	50 (100.00)	200 (100.00)	200 (100.00)

Note: As per Table—6.1.,

Table—6.8: Should à widow be remarried?

Answers	*Brahman*		*Chasa*		*Bauri*		*Santal*		*Total*	
	M	*F*	*M*	*F*	*M*	*F*	*M*	*F*	*M*	*F*
(1)	*(2)*	*(3)*	*(4)*	*(5)*	*(6)*	*(7)*	*(8)*	*(9)*	*(10)*	*(11)*
Yes	8 (16.00)	12 (24.00)	10 (20.00)	11 (22.00)	11 (22.00)	13 (26.00)	48 (96.00)	49 (98.00)	77 (38.5)	84 (42.00)
No	42 (84.00)	38 (76.00)	40 (80.00)	39 (78.00)	39 (78.00)	37 (74.00)	2 (4.00)	1 (2.00)	123 (61.50)	116 (58.00)
Total	50 (100.00)	50 (100.00)	50 (100.00)	50 (100.00)	50 (100.00)	50 (100.00)	50 (100.00)	50 (100.00)	200 (100.00)	200 (100.00)

Note: As per Table—6.1.

Table—6.9: Knowledge of the legal right of women on widow remarriage

Variables	*Brahman*		*Chasa*		*Bauri*		*Santal*		*Total*	
	M	*F*	*M*	*F*	*M*	*F*	*M*	*F*	*M*	*F*
(1)	*(2)*	*(3)*	*(4)*	*(5)*	*(6)*	*(7)*	*(8)*	*(9)*	*(10)*	*(11)*
Have	24 (48.00)	17 (34.00)	15 (30.00)	6 (12.00)	3 (6.00)	–	–	–	39 (19.50)	23 (11.50)
Do not have	26 (52.00)	33 (66.00)	35 (70.00)	44 (88.00)	47 (94.00)	50 (100.00)	50 (100.00)	50 (100.00)	161 (80.50)	177 (88.50)
Total	50 (100.00)	50 (100.00)	50 (100.00)	50 (100.00)	50 (100.00)	50 (100.00)	50 (100.00)	50 (100.00)	200 (100.00)	200 (100.00)

Note: As per Table—6.1.

Table—6.10: Should an unmarried girl adopt a child

Answers	*Brahman*		*Chasa*		*Bauri*		*Santal*		*Total*	
	M	*F*	*M*	*F*	*M*	*F*	*M*	*F*	*M*	*F*
(1)	*(2)*	*(3)*	*(4)*	*(5)*	*(6)*	*(7)*	*(8)*	*(9)*	*(10)*	*(11)*
Yes	–	–	–	–	–	–	–	–	–	–
No	50 (100.00)	50 (100.00)	50 (100.00)	50 (100.00)	50 (100.00)	50 (100.00)	50 (100.00)	50 (100.00)	200 (100.00)	200 (100.00)
Total	50 (100.00)	50 (100.00)	50 (100.00)	50 (100.00)	50 (100.00)	50 (100.00)	50 (100.00)	50 (100.00)	200 (100.00)	200 (100.00)

Note: As per Table—6.1.

Table—6.11: Should a widow adopt a child

Answers	*Brahman*		*Chasa*		*Bauri*		*Santal*		*Total*	
	M	*F*	*M*	*F*	*M*	*F*	*M*	*F*	*M*	*F*
(1)	*(2)*	*(3)*	*(4)*	*(5)*	*(6)*	*(7)*	*(8)*	*(9)*	*(10)*	*(11)*
Yes	7 (14.00)	17 (34.00)	3 (6.00)	7 (14.00)	10 (20.00)	15 (30.00)	2 (4.00)	3 (6.00)	22 (11.00)	42 (21.00)
No	43 (86.00)	33 (66.00)	47 (94.00)	43 (86.00)	40 (80.00)	35 (70.00)	48 (96.00)	47 (94.00)	178 (89.00)	158 (79.00)
Total	50 (100.00)	50 (100.00)	50 (100.00)	50 (100.00)	50 (100.00)	50 (100.00)	50 (100.00)	50 (100.00)	200 (100.00)	200 (100.00)

Note: As per Table—6.1.

Table—6.12: Do you know that as per the Govt. rules, an unmarried girl can adopt a child?

Answers	*Brahman*		*Chasa*		*Bauri*		*Santal*		*Total*	
	M	*F*	*M*	*F*	*M*	*F*	*M*	*F*	*M*	*F*
(1)	*(2)*	*(3)*	*(4)*	*(5)*	*(6)*	*(7)*	*(8)*	*(9)*	*(10)*	*(11)*
Yes	–	–	–	–	–	–	–	–	–	–
No	50 (100.00)	50 (100.00)	50 (100.00)	50 (100.00)	50 (100.00)	50 (100.00)	50 (100.00)	50 (100.00)	200 (100.00)	200 (100.00)
Total	50 (100.00)	50 (100.00)	50 (100.00)	50 (100.00)	50 (100.00)	50 (100.00)	50 (100.00)	50 (100.00)	200 (100.00)	200 (100.00)

Note: As per Table—6.1.

Table—6.13: Do you know that as per the Govt. rules, a widow can adopt a child?

Answers	*Brahman*		*Chasa*		*Bauri*		*Santal*		*Total*	
	M	*F*	*M*	*F*	*M*	*F*	*M*	*F*	*M*	*F*
(1)	*(2)*	*(3)*	*(4)*	*(5)*	*(6)*	*(7)*	*(8)*	*(9)*	*(10)*	*(11)*
Yes	20 (40.00)	11 (22.00)	8 (16.00)	8 (16.00)	3 (6.00)	3 (6.00)	6 (12.00)	2 (1.00)	37 (18.50)	24 (12.00)
No	30 (60.00)	39 (78.00)	42 (84.00)	42 (84.00)	47 (94.00)	47 (94.00)	44 (88.00)	48 (96.00)	163 (81.50)	176 (88.00)
Total	50 (100.00)	50 (100.00)	50 (100.00)	50 (100.00)	50 (100.00)	50 (100.00)	50 (100.00)	50 (100.00)	200 (100.00)	200 (100.00)

Note: As per Table—6.1.

Table—6.14: Whether a person should give dowry on the marriage of his daughter

Answers	*Brahman*		*Chasa*		*Bauri*		*Total*	
	M	*F*	*M*	*F*	*M*	*F*	*M*	*F*
(1)	*(2)*	*(3)*	*(4)*	*(5)*	*(6)*	*(7)*	*(8)*	*(9)*
Yes	24 (48.00)	37 (74.00)	13 (26.00)	8 (16.00)	7 (14.00)	7 (14.00)	44 (29.33)	52 (34.67)
No	26 (52.00)	13 (26.00)	37 (74.00)	42 (84.00)	43 (86.00)	43 (86.00)	106 (70.77)	98 (65.33)
Total	50 (100.00)	50 (100.00)	50 (100.00)	50 (100.00)	50 (100.00)	50 (100.00)	150 (100.00)	150 (100.00)

Note: As per Table—6.1.

Table—6.15: Awareness of prohibition of dowry system

Variables	*Brahman*		*Chasa*		*Bauri*		*Total*	
	M	*F*	*M*	*F*	*M*	*F*	*M*	*F*
(1)	(2)	(3)	(4)	(5)	(6)	(7)	(8)	(9)
Aware	30 (60.00)	18 (36.00)	16 (32.00)	10 (20.00)	6 (12.00)	4 (8.00)	52 (34.67)	32 (21.33)
Unaware	20 (40.00)	32 (64.00)	34 (68.00)	40 (80.00)	44 (88.00)	46 (92.00)	98 (65.33)	118 (78.67)
Total	50 (100.00)	50 (100.00)	50 (100.00)	50 (100.00)	50 (100.00)	50 (100.00)	150 (100.00)	150 (100.00)

Note: As per Table—6.1.

Table—6.16: Awareness of prohibition of medical termination of pregnancy (MTP)

Variables	*Brahman*		*Chasa*		*Bauri*		*Santal*		*Total*	
	M	*F*	*M*	*F*	*M*	*F*	*M*	*F*	*M*	*F*
(1)	*(2)*	*(3)*	*(4)*	*(5)*	*(6)*	*(7)*	*(8)*	*(9)*	*(10)*	*(11)*
Aware	19 (38.00)	20 (40.00)	18 (36.00)	4 (8.00)	–	–	–	–	37 (18.50)	24 (12.00)
Unware	31 (62.00)	30 (60.00)	32 (64.00)	46 (92.00)	50 (100.00)	50 (100.00)	50 (100.00)	50 (100.00)	163 (81.50)	176 (88.00)
Total	50 (100.00)	50 (100.00)	50 (100.00)	50 (100.00)	50 (100.00)	50 (100.00)	50 (100.00)	50 (100.00)	200 (100.00)	200 (100.00)

Note: As per Table—6.1.

Table—6.17: Awareness on the minimum wage fixed by the government of Orissa

Variables	*Brahman*		*Chasa*		*Bauri*		*Santal*		*Total*	
	M	*F*	*M*	*F*	*M*	*F*	*M*	*F*	*M*	*F*
(1)	*(2)*	*(3)*	*(4)*	*(5)*	*(6)*	*(7)*	*(8)*	*(9)*	*(10)*	*(11)*
Aware	18 (36.00)	5 (10.00)	19 (38.00)	4 (8.00)	–	–	2 (4.00)	–	39 (19.50)	9 (4.50)
Unware	32 (64.00)	45 (90.00)	31 (62.00)	46 (92.00)	50 (100.00)	50 (100.00)	48 (96.00)	–	161 (80.50)	191 (95.50)
Total	50 (100.00)	50 (100.00)	50 (100.00)	50 (100.00)	50 (100.00)	50 (100.00)	50 (100.00)	50 (100.00)	200 (100.00)	200 (100.00)

Note: As per the Table—6.1.

Table—6.18: Awareness of the provision of equal wage for equal work

Variables	*Brahman*		*Chasa*		*Bauri*		*Santal*		*Total*	
	M	*F*	*M*	*F*	*M*	*F*	*M*	*F*	*M*	*F*
(1)	*(2)*	*(3)*	*(4)*	*(5)*	*(6)*	*(7)*	*(8)*	*(9)*	*(10)*	*(11)*
Aware	8 (16.00)	–	6 (12.00)	–	–	–	–	–	14 (7.00)	–
Unaware	42 (81.00)	50 (100.00)	44 (88.00)	50 (100.00)	50 (100.00)	50 (100.00)	50 (100.00)	50 (100.00)	186 (93.00)	200 (100.00)
Total	50 (100.00)	50 (100.00)	50 (100.00)	50 (100.00)	50 (100.00)	50 (100.00)	50 (100.00)	50 (100.00)	200 (100.00)	200 (100.00)

Note: As per Table—6.1.

Table—6.19: Awareness of inheritance right of women on paternal properties

Variables	*Brahman*		*Chasa*		*Bauri*		*Santal*		*Total*	
	M	*F*	*M*	*F*	*M*	*F*	*M*	*F*	*M*	*F*
(1)	*(2)*	*(3)*	*(4)*	*(5)*	*(6)*	*(7)*	*(8)*	*(9)*	*(10)*	*(11)*
Aware	31 (62.00)	19 (38.00)	27 (54.00)	17 (34.00)	16 (32.00)	3 (6.00)	6 (12.00)	1 (2.00)	80 (40.00)	40 (20.00)
Unaware	19 (38.00)	31 (62.00)	13 (26.00)	33 (66.00)	34 (68.00)	47 (94.00)	44 (88.00)	49 (98.00)	120 (60.00)	160 (80.00)
Total	50 (100.00)	50 (100.00)	50 (100.00)	50 (100.00)	50 (100.00)	50 (100.00)	50 (100.00)	50 (100.00)	200 (100.00)	200 (100.00)

Note: As per the Table—6.1.

Table—6.20: Whether the wife should have the right to inherit an equal share of paternal property

Answers	*Brahman*		*Chasa*		*Bauri*		*Santal*		*Total*	
	M	*F*	*M*	*F*	*M*	*F*	*M*	*F*	*M*	*F*
(1)	*(2)*	*(3)*	*(4)*	*(5)*	*(6)*	*(7)*	*(8)*	*(9)*	*(10)*	*(11)*
Yes	6 (12.00)	16 (32.00)	7 (14.00)	10 (20.00)	6 (12.00)	6 (12.00)	–	–	19 (9.50)	32 (16.00)
No	44 (88.00)	34 (68.00)	43 (86.00)	40 (80.00)	44 (88.00)	44 (88.00)	50 (100.00)	50 (100.00)	181 (90.50)	168 (84.00)
Total	50 (100.00)	50 (100.00)	50 (100.00)	50 (100.00)	50 (100.00)	50 (100.00)	50 (100.00)	50 (100.00)	200 (100.00)	200 (100.00)

Note: As per Table—6.1.

7

Summary and Conclusion

Summary of Findings

Men and women are thought to be the two sides of the same coin but it is irrefutable to say that they are considered as equal. Since very remote past, women have been considered as an underclass in many countries of the world, particularly in India. And nowadays their problem in relation to 'gender discrimination' has become a radical social issue which is aggravating at an alarming rate throughout the country, since, even to-day, after more than 52 years of independence of our country discrimination against them still persists in all major socio-economic domains of daily life. They are to bear all sorts of discrimination and lead a restricted lifestyle as per the wish or desire of the male members of their family or of the society as a whole at the larger front.

In order to eradicate this social disparity, government has formulated various constitutional measures and have enacted a number of legislative measures at different points of time depending upon the arousal of varied problems. But even then, no significant change is marked, rather in most of the cases their social status has remained unchanged or in some cases their position is witnessed to be deteriorating. As for example, the problem of dowry and dowry deaths may be referred to which were not occurring so rampantly during few decades ago. However, it is mainly because of high illiteracy among the female and unsatisfactory or ill-conditioned movement of the government in creating awareness generation among the general mass on the social privileges and welfare measures made available for them and the punishments legally sanctioned for the deviants.

However, in India, we have a distinct social system based on the principles of fore-fold *Varna* organisation [i.e. Brahman (prist), Kshyatriya (warrior), Vaishya (trader) and Shudra (artisan)], by which specificity as compared to others in relation to its social norms, values and cultural practices. In this respect the social status of women of one *Varna* is not necessarily the same as of the women of other *Varnas*. So, in the present piece of research, an attempt has been made to unfold a comprehensive review of the present social status of the Indian women belonging to different social segments of the caste hierarchy, i.e. upper caste Hindus, such as Brahman, Hindu peasants (Chasa or farming caste), ex-untouchable (Bauris or agricultural labourers) and the Scheduled Tribes (Santal, or immigrant forest dwelling population to Bhubaneswar city who mainly work as wage-earners).

The present study has been conducted in five multi-caste Hindu villages located on the outskirts of Bhubaneswar city and two slums falling within the Municipal limits of the city. All the study villages as well as the slums belong to Bhubaneswar block of Khurdha district. Since these villages and slums fall in and around the Bhubaneswar city, the State capital of Orissa, people belonging to the study areas have better access to various amenities, like educational institutions, public health centres and hospitals, post offices, transport system, government offices, law courts etc. and have better exposure to various mass media.

The broad aims and objectives of the study are to find out (i) the notion of culturally determined mode of behaviour for male and female children, (ii) the educational deprivation of the girl child and the associated socio-cultural factors thereof, (iii) the culture of diet and eating pattern related to the girl child and a boy child, (iv) the level of discrimination on health sector in relation to preferential treatment process and, (v) the levels of awareness of men and women about the protective measures and their views. The last or the sixth objectives is to formulate a model of action plan for the well-being of the girl children and the women.

The result of the study is based on the information obtained from a total sample of 200 male and 200 female informants taken from 200 households (viz. Brahman, Chasa, Bauri and Santal, 50 each).

The executive summary findings are as follows:

(a) Education and Gender

(i) Educationally women are very backward as compared to their male counterparts in all the four communities studied. But, the percentage of literacy of Brahman women (70.27) is more than that of the Chasa (42.86), Santal (28.42) and Bauri women (24.74) as against 91.23 per cent of Brahman, 61.07 per cent of Chasa, 57.6 per cent of Bauri and 53.27 per cent of Santal men who are literate.

(ii) There are 42 Brahman, 67 Chasa, 74 Bauri and 54 Santal men as against 36, 68, 49 and 53 women of the respective communities in 3 important age groups, viz, 5-9, 10-19 and 20-24 in which people normally attain formal education. But as compared to men, there are much less women in each of the study communities who are now continuing their education in different classes.

There are 71.43 per cent of Brahman men as against only 44.44 per cent of women of this community who are now continuing their studies. Amongst the Chasa when more than 50 per cent (52.24) of men continuing their education, there are less than 25 per cent of (23.53) women who are following them. So far as the case of Bauri and Santal people is concerned it seems to be very grim since of the total female population of these two communities falling under the said age groups, only 14.29 per cent of Bauri and 4.43 per cent of Santal women are found to be continuing their education as against 44.59 per cent of Bauri and 37.04 per cent of Santal men.

(iii) In order to find out gender discrimination in relation to availing of an educational opportunity, a question relating to a probable situation was put to the parents. The situation was like this: 'Suppose you have 1 children, 2 sons and 2 daughters and government would provide education with all possible facilities, that is, free education only to 2 of them. In that case whom do you prefer?' Surprisingly most of the Santal (66.00%), Chasa (62.00%) and Bauri (54.00%) as against 42 per cent Brahman preferred to avail the opportunity for both of their sons and there was no amongst them who said that he/she would avail the opportunity for both of their daughters. Other respondents opted to avail the opportunity for one son and one daughter. This certainly indicates that so far as education is concerned female children are highly discriminated as against male children. However, when a subsequent question in relation to availing of an employment opportunity for only one child of the two educated children was put to the parents; about 79 per cent of Chasa, 77 per cent of Santal, 74 per cent of Bauri and 66 per cent of Brahman told that they would avail the employment opportunity for their son only, whereas the rest of the respondents said that they would choose those children irrespective of sex who are more qualified and fit for the concerned job. There was nobody in any of the communities who had wanted to avail the said employment opportunity in favour of his/her daughter. This is because in patrilocal societies, daughters are to leave their natal home and live with their affinal kins after their marriage. Thus, their income goes to the hands of their husbands or parents-in-law but never comes to the hands of their own parents.

(iv) So far as the factors responsible for dwindling literacy among the females of these communities are concerned, as many as 13 multiple reasons are found to be there. These are: poor economic condition of parents (58.64%), helping parents in economic and daily household pursuits (30.25%), unproductive expenditure (30.25%), attaining adulthood/ marriageable age (29.01%), looking after younger siblings during absence or working hours of parents (28.4%), engagement in activities involved with earning of cash or kind at an early age (20.99%), problem of searching educated grooms for educated brides (17.28%), looking after diseased parents or death of parents (14.20%), failure in class promotion (7.41%), disapproval of society (4.94%) and fear of teachers (1.85%).

(b) Culture of Food Consumption and the Women

Culture of food consumption is an important social aspect in status identification between male and female persons of Indian traditional societies. Since in such societies the male members are highly respected and their authority is recognised by the females as per the go of the society, they are served food first and preferably the females consume their share after the male members have their food.

The present study reveals that in 86 per cent of Chasa as against 84 per cent of Brahman, 74 per cent of Bauri and 62 per cent of Santal households, the male and female members do not sit together for lunch or supper when all the family members are present rather in these households the male members are served food before the females consume the same.

(c) Health, Treatment of Diseases and the Women

(i) Presently 33.04 per cent of Santal, 30 per cent of Bauri, 17 per cent of Brahman and 15.75 per cent of Chasa females as against 33.87 per cent of Santal, 28.47 per cent of Bauri, 26.09 per cent of Chasa and 14.75 per cent of Brahman males are suffering from various diseases. But comparatively much less percentage of women of each community are undergoing medical treatment. The study shows that out of the total diseased persons 64.64 per cent of Brahman, 50 per cent of Chasa, 31.58 per cent of Santal and 27.27 per cent of Bauri women are presently undergoing medical treatment as against 77.78, 63.88, 52.38 and 43.58 per cent of men of the respective communities.

(ii) So far as the type of treatment among the diseased men and women who are undergoing medical treatment in all the communities excepting Santal is concerned, more number of diseased men than diseased women are undergoing allopathic treatment. It has been witnessed that there are 73.91 per cent of Chasa, 64.29 per cent of Brahman, 64.71 per cent of Bauri men as against 57.14 per cent of Brahman, 50 per cent of Chasa and 33.33 per cent of Bauri women, who are undergoing this type of treatment. Among the Bauri (66.67%), Chasa (50.00%) and Brahman (42.86%), there are more diseased women who are undergoing homeopathic treatment which is cheaper. There are very few men belonging to Brahman and Chasa communities who are undergoing Ayurvedic treatment and there is not a single woman in any community who is undergoing this kind of treatment.

(d) Occupation, Utilization of Income and the Women

(i) Most of the women of lower castes who are poor, work as wage-earners but they do not normally possess ownership right on what they earn.

(ii) Majority of the female spouses of Brahman (98%) and Chasa (92%) as against only 10 per cent of Bauri and 14 per cent of Santal communities are engaged in housekeeping activities, but as many as 86 per cent of Bauri and 82 per cent of Santal female spouses work as wage-earners. There are 2 female spouses in each of the Bauri (4%), Santal (4%), and Chasa (6%) communities who run some petty business and earn some cash to supplement their family-income. One

(2%) Brahman lady is a service holder and their is non in any of the rest three communities who earns from this source of income.

(iii) So far as the management of the earnings of the female spouses is concerned, a concrete picture comes into the right. The only Brahman woman who is employed says that a major part of her monthly income is given to her husband and she keeps a small portion of it for her daily expenses. But all the 4 Chasa women who earn either from petty business or wage-earning say that the whole amount of their earning is given to their husbands. However, a different picture is observed to be happening among the Bauri and Santal. Of the total Bauri and Santal women engaged in earning cash, 55.56 per cent of Bauri as against 60.47 per cent of Santal say that they handover their whole income to their respective husbands and the rest percentage of women say that they keep the whole amount of money they earn with themselves and manage home but certainly they do so as per the will of the husbands.

(iv) If the working women do not give the money earned by themselves to their respective husbands or do not utilise the money according to their wish, the consequence becomes very bitter. Most of the women (83.87%) of all the communities taken together say that in case they do not give their earnings to their husbands, the latter snatch away the same by applying physical force. But 37.78 per cent of Bauri women, which is 18.28 per cent of the total working women of all the four communities taken together say that if they resist their husbands they are threatened with dire consequences.

(e) Legislative Measures and the Women

(i) In order to empower the women and eradicate gender discrimination, constitution of India has equated all

citizens irrespective of sex under various fundamental rights proclaimed under different Articles. Some of the important Articles that are more or less women specific are: Art. 14, Art. 15, Art. 16, Art. 39, Art. 40, Art. 41, Art. 42, Art. 43, Art. 44, Art. 45, Art. 47, Art. 325, Art. 520, etc. These Articles are related to freedom of speech, expression, residence, occupation, public assistance, exploitation, religion, property, education, election on the basis of adult franchise, nutrition and public health. However, apart from these constitutional provisions, various legislative measures have also been made by the government at different points of time in order to fulfil the constitutional goals in relation to the upliftment of women of our country. The important legislative, social and economic measures that have been taken up are the Child Marriage Restraint Act, 1929; the Special Marriage Act, 1954; the Hindu Marriage Act, 1955; the Special Marriage Act, 1955; the Hindu Adoption and Maintenance Act, 1956; the Hindu Succession Act, 1956; the Dowry Prohibition Act, 1961; the Maternity Benefit Act, 1961; the Special Marriage Act, 1964; the Medical Termination of Pregnancy (MTP) Act, 1971; the Equal Remuneration Act, 1978; the Immortal Traffic (Prevention) Act, 1956; the Indecent Representation of Women (Prohibition Act, 1986 and the Commission of *Sati* (Prevention) Act, 1987). Under these Acts various interests of Indian women are legally protected and hence a person going against any of these provisions is punishable under law. But the awareness of the public, especially women on these legal provisions is very poor which is mainly because of their illiteracy, low exposure to modern mass-media and initiation of action programmes of the government on providing awareness generation to such people at a very low-key.

(f) Protective Measures and the Women

In order to assess the level of awareness, some important questions were put to the sample population, particularly parents on the following issues:

— Age at marriage;

— Selection of mate and right to divorce;

— Widow remarriage and adoption of child;

— Dowry prohibition;

— Medical termination of pregnancy (MTP;

— Inheritance and disposal of property; and

— Equal wage opportunity for equal work.

(i) A total number of 39 men accounting for 19.5 per cent as against only 21 or 10.5 per cent of women irrespective of any community are found to be aware of the minimum age fixed for marriage of a girl. However, when 54 per cent of Brahman men as against 34 per cent of Brahman women possess knowledge on this, the awareness level of Bauri and Santal people is almost nil since there are only 3 (6.00%) men and 1 (2.00) woman of Santal community as against only 1 (2.00%) Bauri man who are found to be aware about this matter. So far as the level of awareness about the minimum age prescribed for marriage of a man is concerned, the trend is also almost the same.

(ii) That 34 per cent of men as against 45 per cent of women of the total sample say that a girl should have the right to choose her life partner but when highest percentage of men and women of Santal community say like this, there are lowest percentage of men and women among the Brahman community who are of the same opinion. But there is not a single man or woman in any of the four communities who is of the opinion that she should have the right to choose her life partner outside her caste, sub-caste, community

or religion. However, there are very few percentage of men (18.5) and women (10.00%) who are aware that legally a girl can marry a person outside her caste, sub-caste, community or religion.

(iii) A total number of 41 men and 51 women accounting for 20.50 and 25.50 per cent respectively of the total sample are of the opinion that the wife should have the right to divorce her husband for the same reasons a husband divorces his wife but the rest percentage of people say that she should not have this right since they are economically dependent on their husbands and hence they would be helpless if they would do so. However, highest percentage of Santal men (36.00%) and women (62.00%) as compared to other communities favour the idea that the wife should have the right to divorce her husband for the same reasons a husband would divorce his wife since in their society the women are economically more independent than the women of other communities.

So far as the awareness of the people on the legal right of the women on the above matter is concerned, irrespective of any community, there are 36 or 18 per cent of men as against 15 or 7.5 per cent of women who have knowledge about this matter. But comparatively there are more percentage of men and women in Brahman community who are aware that legally the women are empowered to divorce their husbands for the same reasons, their husbands would divorce them.

(iv) Widow remarriage is a critical issue in Hindu society. In this regard when a question relating to remarriage of a widow was put, most of the Brahman men (84%) and women (76%) as against 80 per cent of Chasa men and 78 per cent of women, 78 per cent of Bauri men and 74 per cent of women say that a widow should not remarry. But, on the contrary, as many as 48 or 96 per cent of Santal men as against 49 or 98 per cent of women maintain that such a person

should remarry since by doing this, one would not commit any sin. However, there are as many as 161 or 80.50 per cent of men as against 177 or 88.5 per cent of women who do not know that as per the legal provision, a widow is entitled to remarry. So far as the case of the individual communities is concerned, it is found that there are 48 per cent of Brahman men and 34 per cent of women, as against 30 per cent of Chasa men and 12 per cent of women, who have knowledge about this legal provision. But there is none in Santal community as against only 3 or 6 per cent of Bauri men who know that as per the legal provision a widow is permitted to remarry.

(v) So far as the legal provision relating to adoption of child by an unmarried women is concerned, there is nobody in any of the four communities who is in favour of the fact that such a person should adopt a child. Similarly there is nobody who is aware of the legal provision that such a person can adopt a child. However, of the total sample, there are 18.5 per cent of men as against 12 per cent of women who have knowledge on the matter that a widow can adopt a child.

(vi) Of the total sample, there are 70.76 per cent of men as against 65.33 per cent of women who are of the opinion that a person should not give any dowry on the marriage of his/her daughter. But comparatively there are more percentage of Brahman men (48.00) and women (74.00) as against 26 per cent of Chasa men and 16 per cent of Chasa women and 14 per cent of Bauri men and women who say that a person should give dowry on the marriage occasion of his/her daughter. However, there are about 65 per cent of men as against 79 per cent of women who are unaware that legally giving or receiving of dowry in any form is an offence and hence punishable under law. The level of awareness of Brahman men (60%) and women (36%) is much higher than those of the Chasa and Bauri communities.

(vii) Awareness about the legal prohibition of medical termination of pregnancy (MTP) is very poor among the public. There is not a single man or woman neither in Bauri community nor in Santal community who is aware of this matter. However, there are 38 per cent of Brahman men and 40 per cent of women as against 36 per cent Chasa men and 8 per cent women, who are found to have knowledge on this matter. Out of the total population of all the four communities, the percentage of men and women who are unaware of this legislation come to be 18.5 per cent and 88 respectively.

(viii) The provision of equal wage for equal work is a very important social reform towards uplifting the condition of women workers. But practically this provision is not well known among the general mass. There are only 8 or 16 per cent of Brahman men as against 6 or 12 per cent of Chasa men, together accounting for 7 per cent of the whole sample, are found to be aware of this matter and the rest are still unaware. However, there are 19 or 19.50 per cent of men and 9 or 4.5 per cent of women who know about the minimum wage fixed for the unskilled workers by the government. Surprisingly there is not a single Bauri man or woman who has knowledge on this matter. Among the Santals, there are only 2 men who are aware of the minimum wage fixed by the government. On the contrary as compared to these people, there are more number of Brahman and Chasa men and women who are aware of this piece of information.

(ix) Of the total sample, 9.5 per cent of men as against 16 per cent of women maintain that the wife should have the right to inherit an equal share of paternal property but practically there are 60 per cent of men and 80 per cent of women who do not know that as per the government provision a wife can have an equal share of her paternal poverty along with her siblings. However, compared to the Bauri and Santal men and

women there are more Brahman and Chasa men and women who are aware of this provision.

Concluding Remarks

Educationally women of all the communities are very backward than men. This is because traditionally they are considered as if they are born only to bear children and look after the daily chores of domestic life. The traditional systems of authority, lineage and locality of residence of spouses also greatly influence the educational status of women. As the Brahman, Chasa, Bauri and Santal people are mainly patriarchal, patrilineal and patrilocal in nature, parents do not like to spend much money on the education of their daughters rather give much stress on how they should know the art of home management that they think is the most important task for women.

- In most of the cases women are considered as an underclass, and they themselves also consider their male counterparts as superior beings. So they respect and obey them. Even they do not take food before the male members have consumed their share, particularly the family head is fed.
- Most of the women of Scheduled Caste and tribal communities, like Bauri and Santal work as wage-earners but they do not possess ownership right on what they earn. Even in many caste Hindu communities like Brahman and Chasa, the income earned by women workers or salaried service-holder, goes straight to the hands of their respective husbands and if the women resist their husbands by denying to hand over their income to them, they are physically and mentally harassed, otherwise they are threatened with dire consequences, like legal separation. This compels the women to simply remain as subservient to men, particularly to their husbands.
- The level of awareness on different social legislative measures is very poor, particularly among the non-literate public mass. However, more men and women

of upper caste Hindu communities, like Brahman are better aware of some of such measures than the lower caste Hindu communities and, Scheduled Caste or tribal communities, like Bauri and Santal. This is because, economically, educationally as well as culturally such people are more advanced than the latter and have greater exposure to various modern mass media.

However, the inequalities persisting between the sexes would not be completely eradicated from any society unless the people become conscious that men and women are like the two sides of the same coin and hence equal leading of life without the other sex is absolutely impossible and cannot be thought of in any manner. However, the role of the government agencies and NGOs seem to be very important. No doubt, government has brought about many social reforms by enacting various legislative measures at various points of time for the upliftment of the girl children and women, but simply enacting such measures does not mean anything unless the public know about them and become conscious of their rights, privileges and the punishment legally sanctioned for the deviants.

Suggestive Measures

(a) India is a very big country with diversified ethno-cultural groups spreading over various cultural zones of the country. Since culture together with ecological conditions plays a very vital role in building of ones personality and educational career, emphasis must be laid on formulation of specific need-based educational programmes pertaining to girls rather than by universalising similar programmes uniformly all over the country without giving importance to cultures.

(b) In order to raise the level of literacy among the women, sufficient interest must be created among the parents, especially among the poorer communities, by the way of providing the following special economic benefits:

(i) Socio-economically backward parents consider that spending money on the education of girl

children is a matter of spoiling the scarce resources that have with them since such children are subjected to change their natal residence permanently after their marriage to their affine's home. Hence, they are not considered as economically productive for their parents. In order to tackle this reality, identification of poor parents below the poverty line and providing free education to the girl children with all other facilities on priority basis would be taken up. This would be a very fruitful action programme for raising the literacy of girls, especially among the poor communities.

(ii) Apart from the above suggestion, provision should also be made to provide additional quota of ration to those poor parents who send their girl children to schools or to any other educational institution. However, distribution of additional quota of ration must be of different quantities depending upon the levels of education of the girl children of a household, as for example, if the amount of the additional quota of ration, say rice or wheat, be 100 gram per girl child who is educated upto primary level, it should be 150 or 200 grams if she completes middle level education and so on so forth. However, if for the time being, it is not possible as it would be burdensome for the government, some strict steps may also be taken, like legalising compulsory education for all irrespective of sex, and punishment may be imposed by way of reducing the normal quofa of ration for the defaulting parents who do not send their girl children to school.

(iii) There should be job guarantee for the female matriculates belonging to destitute or poor families falling below the poverty line or need-based vocational training be provided to them depending upon the demand of the market and interest of the trainees. However, the fact lies on

the nature of income of the educated women. As per the tradition discussed earlier, women, leave their parents after their marriage and permanently reside with their husbands at their in-law's home. Such married women look to their future along with their husbands and children but not with their parents. As a result, the earning of the educated women, if employed or engaged in self entrepreneurship, goes directly to the hands of their husbands and no part of it comes to the hands of their parents. This system is found to be the most important reason for which the parents lack interest to educate their girl children. This attitude of parents should be changed by mobilising public opinion.

(c) As per the laws relating to inheritance of equal share of paternal property by daughters, a girl is entitled to exercise her right in this regard. But practically exercising of this right by the intending girls involves various social problems that normally leads to break up of the social ties between married daughters and their respective natal families. As for example, if as per the legal provision, a married woman demands to have her share of parental property, suddenly all her brothers treat her and her affines as their enemy and once the sister succeeds in getting her share, the social tie between these two group of kins is likely to get cut off for ever. But by nature human is a social being and he/she lives in society with his/her consanguineal and affinal kins of various degrees, and as such, he/she does not like to break up any relationship with any of his/her relatives. In this context, with a view to avoid the above problem, which arises when a married woman asks for her share of paternal property, provision must be made in an accepted manner to give a girl her share of the property at the time of her marriage with pleasure. This would certainly create a consciousness among

men to consider women as equal with them and as such they would be mentally prepared to handover the due share of their sisters to them without any problem. By doing this the social relationship between the two parties would remain pleasant.

(d) It is very true that the legal provisions relating to age at marriage, right to select mate by the girls, right of women to divorce their husbands on the same grounds that they would be divorced by their husbands, right of a widow to remarry, adoption of children by widows and unmarried women, dowry prohibition, medical termination of pregnancy etc. are some of the very important tasks before the government to mitigate the condition of women, and hence, thereby equalise them with them. But practically most of the people, particularly those belonging to socio-economically backward communities are not aware of these social reforms made in the country after independence by the popular government. So, government must take up some concrete steps to popularise the legal provisions available for women. It would take up the help of various media like, television, radio, newspapers, magazines, journals, etc. to propagate the said provisions on priority basis. However, much emphasis need be given on propagation of these provisions through all the private and public television channels available in the country since television has nowadays reached to many areas. The electronic audio-visual media have greater impact on the public as it provides both audio and visual realities. However, strict rules be made for all the media, particularly television, radio and newspapers to popularise government reforms and programmes in respect of girl children and women free of cost. Apart from this, NGOs must also take some positive initiatives to work in this field rather than concentrating on only economic development or other such action programmes.

Appendix-A

NABAKRUSHNA CHOUDHURY CENTRE FOR DEVELOPMENT STUDIES, ORISSA, BHUBANESWAR-751013

"Status and empowerment of the girl child and the women in contemporary (Oriya) caste Hindu societies—A Cross—Cultural Study".

1. Name of the village:
2. Ward:
3. Caste/Tribe:
4. Sub-caste/Sub-Tribe:
5. Gotra/Clan:
6. Religion:
7. Mother Tongue:
8. Language Known:
9. Nature of Society:
   (a) Patriarchal/Matriarchal
   (b) Patrilineal/Matrilineal
   (c) Patrilocal/Matrilocal
   (d) Patronymic/Matronymic
10. Land holding pattern of the household

A. (i) Total agricultural land

(ii) Total homestead land

B. (i) Total agricultural land available in the name of the female members of the households

(ii) Total homestead land available in the name of the female members of the household

C. Why most of the land are recorded in the name of the male members?

11. Household census

Sl. No.	*Name*	*Rel. with head*	*Age*	*Sex*	*M. stat.*	*Age at M*	*Occupation P*	*Occupation S*	*Edn.*	*C/D/O/ N.E.*	*Factors of D.O/ N.E.*
(1)	(2)	(3)	(4)	(5)	(6)	(7)	(8)	(9)	(10)	(11)	(12)
1.											
2.											
3.											
4.											
5.											
6.											
7.											
8.											
9.											
10.											

M–Marriage, C–Continuing, D–Drop out, N.E–Not enrolled, P–Primary, S–Subsidiary.

12. Culture and gender biasness

(a) What was your first desired 'child'? (M/F).

(i) If a male child, why?

(ii) If not a female child, why?

(b) As per your opinion, what is the ideal number of children a couple should have? 1, 2, 3, or more.

(i) If only one, its sex and why?

(ii) If only two, their sex/es and why?

(iii) If three, their sex/es and why?

(c) Do you have any device/technique by which you can know the sex of your baby before birth? Yes/No.

(i) If yes, please describe.

(ii) If you know it to be a boy child, what are the taboos you follow for the welfare of the baby?

(iii) If you know it to be a girl child, what are the taboos you follow for the welfare of the child?

(d) Have you ever gone to a medical practitioner to know the gender of your child? Yes/No.

(e) Have you ever terminated the pregnancy medically after knowing the gender of the baby? Yes/No.

(f) Your expectation from your children

(i) eldest son;

(ii) other son/s;

(iii) eldest daughter;

(iv) other daughter/s

13. Gender educational and occupational discrimination

(a) Suppose you have 4 children; two sons and two daughters and the Govt. wants to provide free education with all the facilities, like lodging and boarding free of cost only to two of them. In that case whom do you choose?

(i) both sons and why?

(ii) both daughters and why?

(iii) one son and one daughter and why?

(b) After providing free education, Govt. would provide employment to only one of them. In that case whom you would like to get employed and why.

14. Culture, Food and Heath Status of Family Members

 (a) Do all the male and female members of your family sit together for lunch/supper during the availability of all members? Yes/No.

  (i) If yes—frequently, occasionally and in few cases.

  (ii) If no, please name the persons who are served food first and the reasons thereof.

  (iii) Who take/s food last and why?

 (b) Please name the persons who are suffering/have suffered from any illness recently and the steps taken up for treatment.

Sl. No.	Name	Relation	Illness	Steps taken
1.				
2.				
3.				

15. Consciousness on occupational rights and equal wage rate

Persons	*Equal wage for equal or similar work irrespective of sex*	*Yes/ No.*	*Present amount of wage rate declared by Govt.*	*Yes/No (Amount)*

16. Whether you keep your income with self or give it to your husband?

 (i) Keeps with self

 (ii) Gives to husband

17. If you do not give it to your husband what happens?

 (i) takes by force

 (ii) beats

 (iii) scolds

18. What should be the actual age of a girl and a boy to set married

Persons	Wife	Hu
Boy		
Girl		

19. Do you know the minimum age prescribed for marriage by the Govt?

Persons	Wife	Hu
Wife		
Husband		

20. Do you think that a girl should have the right to choose her life partner?
    - *(i)* Wife (Yes/No)
    - *(ii)* Husband (Yes/No)

21. Do you know that as per the Govt. rules, a girl can select her own life partner outside her caste, sub-caste, community or even religion?
    - *(i)* Wife (Yes/No)
    - *(ii)* Husband (Yes/No)

22. Do you think that the wife should have the right to divorce her husband for the same reasons a husband divorces his wife.
    - *(i)* Wife (Yes/No)
    - *(ii)* Husband (Yes/No)

23. Should a widow be remarried?
    - *(i)* Wife (Yes/No), if no why?
    - *(ii)* Husband (Yes/No), if no why?

24. As per your opinion should an unmarried girl or a widow adopt a child?
    - *(i)* Wife (Yes/No), if no why?

(ii) Husband (Yes/No), if no why?

25. Do you know that as per the government rules, such persons (an unmarried girl or a widow) can adopt a child?

    (i) Wife (Yes/No)

    (ii) Husband (Yes/No)

26. As per your opinion, should a person give dowry for the marriage of his daughter?

    (i) Wife (Yes/No)

    (ii) Husband (Yes/No)

27. (i) Dowry items brought for self

    Dowry items given in daughter's marriage

28. What are the merits of dowry system?

    (i) Wife

    (ii) Husband

29. What are the demerits of dowry system?

    (i) Wife

    (ii) Husband

30. Do you know that government prohibit giving or taking dowry as it is considered as an offence?

    (i) Wife (Yes/No)

    (ii) Husband (Yes/No)

31. Should the wife have the right to inherit equal share of husband's property?

    (i) Wife (Yes/No), if yes, why?

    (ii) Husband (Yes/No), if no, why?

32. Do you know that as per the government rules inheritance of affinal property by wife is practicable?

    (i) Wife (Yes/No)

    (ii) Husband (Yes/No)

33. Should the girls have the right to inherit equal share of paternal property?
    - *(i)* Wife (Yes/No)
    - *(ii)* Husband (Yes/No)
34. In case a daughter gets a share of her paternal property, should have the absolute right to dispose it off in any manner she likes?
    - *(i)* Wife (Yes/No)
    - *(ii)* Husband (Yes/No)
35. In case a widow/wife inherits affinal property, should she have the absolute right to dispose it off in any manner she likes?
    - *(i)* Wife (Yes/No)
    - *(ii)* Husband (Yes/No)
36. Do you know the provision of equal wage for equal or similar work undertaken by men or women?
    - *(i)* Wife (Yes/No)
    - *(ii)* Husband (Yes/No)
37. Do you know the present wage fixed by the government?
    - *(i)* Wife (Yes/No)
    - *(ii)* Husband (Yes/No)
38. Has any female member of your family been illtreated in respect of sexual violence? Yes/No.
39. Do you know that ill treatment in respect of sexual violence is punishable under law? Yes/No.
    - *(i)* Wife (Yes/No)
    - *(ii)* Husband (Yes/No)
40. Are you more attached to your daughter than son/s, if, no why?
41. Why the wife is called as '*Dharma-patni*'?

42. Why the husband is not called as *'Dharma-pati'*?

43. Is it necessary that the wife should maintain her chastity? Yes/No.

    (i) If yes, why?

    (ii) If no, why?

44. Is it necessary that a husband should be truthful to her wife? Yes/No.

    If no, why?

45. Which of the following fastings are observed by a girl/women of your family and why?

    (a) Savitri

    (b) Khudurukuni

    (c) Bhudei osa

    (d) Janhi osa

    (e) Sathi osa

    (f) Bali trutiya

    (g) Dutiya osa

    (h) Naga chaturthi

    (i) Kanjianla

    (j) Chaiti Mangalbar

    (k) Rai Damodar brata

    (l) Banchuka

    (m) Sudasa brata

    (n) Any other (Pl. specify)

46. Is there any fasting (*brata*) observed by the men for the welfare of wife or the family members? Yes/No.

    If yes, what are these?

Appendix–2

EDUCATIONAL AND MEDICAL FACILITIES AVAILABLE IN STUDY VILLAGES

Sl. No	*Villages*	*Educational institutions*	*Year of establishment*	*Appx. distance from the village (in Km)*	*Nearest public health centres (PHCs)*	*Appx. distance from the village (in Km)*	*Nearest hospital*	*Appx. distance from the village*
(1)	*(2)*	*(3)*	*(4)*	*(5)*	*(6)*	*(7)*	*(8)*	*(9)*
1.	Kalarahanga	Kalarahanga Centre Primary School	1910	0	Patia	2 Kms.	Unit-6 Bhubaneswar	11 Kms.
2.	Raghunathpur	Raghunathpur U.G.M.E. School,	1917	0	Baranga	6 Kms.	Unit-6 Bhubaneswar	15 Kms.
		Dadhiban High School	1997	0				
		Kunjabihari Mahvidyalaya Baranga	1978	6				

(Contd...)

(1)	(2)	(3)	(4)	(5)	(6)	(7)	(8)	(9)
3.	Khairapada	Khairapada Primary School,	1903	0	Baranga	5 Kms.	Unit-6 BBSR	20 Kms.
		Utkalmani Ucha Vidyapitha,	1988	0			S.C.B Medical College, Cuttack	20 Kms.
		Utkalmani Balika Ucha Vidyapitha,	1988	0				
		Barang College, Barang	–	4				
4.	Barimund	Barimund L.P School,	1914	0	Gandarpur	4 Kms.	Unit-6 BBSR	22 Kms.
		Barimund M.E School,	1965	0			S.C.B. Medical College Cuttack.	
		Bapujee Vidyapitha	1981	0				
5.	Daruthenga	Daruthenga U.P. School,	1914	0	Mendasal	7 Kms.	Unit-6 BBSR	25 Kms.
		Daruthenga M.E. School,	1962	0				
		Daruthenga High School,	1984	0				
		Jujhagada Primary School	1962	0				
		Kunjabihari Mahavidyalaya	1978	7				

Appendix-3

Case Study–1

Anusuya is the second daughter of Bishnu Prasad Rath of Daruthenga. She is about 18-years-old and Brahman by caste. She has three sisters and one brother. She is educated only upto class two.

She has successfully completed her secondary education but unfortunately she is not now continuing higher education even if she is very interested for study and her father is a well-to-do person. She says that all her sisters including herself are discriminated against their brother as the latter one is given preference in almost all matters. Her parents have a big dream for their son as he would be helpful to them during their old age. She claims that she was forced to discontinue her education since her parents did not pay any attention towards her interest in education. However, she explains that her parents would face a lot of problem if they had allowed her to get higher education since nowadays finding out an educated grooms for educated girls is too difficult. If at all this problem is solved then her parents would also fall in a great difficulty to arrange heavy dowry which is normally demanded by educated grooms.

Case Study–2

Mala Bhoi, an unmarried girl of about 20-years-old resides with her parents in the village of Raghunathpur. She is Bauri

(SC) by caste. She has two brothers; one elder and one younger. Her parents earn their livelihood out of wage-earning.

Mala is an illiterate girl but her elder brother (25) is educated upto 9th class. Her father has spent a lot of hard-earned money on the education of her brother with a hope that he would get employed and help her father during his old-age. But the hope of her father has remained unfulfilled. Mala says that she was very interested to get educated as one of her peers was regularly going to the village school during her childhood. One day when she asked her parents about her admission in the school, her mother became very violent and told in anger that getting educated is not the job of girls; it is the job of the boys and as a girl, she must learn the art of cooking and other household duties as these would be helpful to her when she gets married. Now Mala feels that if she had been educated, she would have been employed and thus be self independent as her friend is.

Case Study–3

Sushama Rath is a Brahman housewife. She is about 32-years-old and is a mother of two girl children. She is educated only upto clans seventh and her husband is a matriculate.

As a Brahman, Sushama leads a very strict social life. She is obedient to her parents-in-law. She feeds them and her husband in time and takes her own food after all of them have taken food. In no case she is permitted to take her food before her father-in-law has consumed. As an orthodox Brahman Hindu, her father-in-law sacrifices the food to the god before he consumes the same. Thereafter, she feeds her mother-in-law. She confesses that this type of dealing is now outdated but she has to follow the tradition since her parents-in-law are very tradition-bound and rigid in nature. Hence, she has no alternative than to act according to the wish of her parents-in-law. However, she says that she is permitted by her husband to take her food whenever she feels hungry. But practically if she takes her food before the senior members of the family have finished their food, she is severely humiliated by her mother-in-law.

Case Study–4

Bina is the only daughter of her parents. She is Chasa by caste and an illiterate. She has one brother. She is 15-year-old and her brother is 19-year-old. Her parents earn their livelihood out of share cultivation as well as wage-earning.

Bina says that as a girl she has to do a lot of household works, such as cleaning of house floor, washing clothes of all the family members, cooking and serving food to them and cleaning of utensils daily. She consumes the remnants of her father and brother. However, she argues that as a girl she must do these activities since these are specific to the female sex and more essential for the unmarried girls as learning household activities and house management at parent's house becomes very easy for one to manage the house of parents-in-law after marriage. However, she further says that she is often scolded for her minutest mistakes while her brother is very loved by her parents and not punished for major mistakes done by him.

When a question regarding her education was put to her she told that for a girl learning of household activities is more important than obtaining of formal educational degrees. Thus, this type of socialisation process reduces the status of females both in familial and community levels as well.

Case Study–5

Bilasa Bhoi is about 37-years-old. She is married and has one son. She is Bauri (SC) by caste. She lives with her husband and son in the village of Raghunathpur.

Both Bilasa and her husband earn their livelihood as wage-earners. But Bilasa says that she earns, still then she does not enjoy any right on her own earnings. She gives whatever she earns to her husband otherwise she is scolded and even severely beaten up. She is often threatened to get divorced. All these she has to resist as her parents have no ability to economically support her if she is divorced and resides with them.

Bibliography

Agarwal, C.M., 1993, *Dimensions of Indian Womanhood*, Almora: Shri Almora Book Depot.

Agarwal, Sushila, 1988, *Status of Women*, Jaipur: Print Well Publishers.

Ahuja, Ram, 1992, *Rights of Women—A Feministic Perspective*. New Delhi: Rawat.

Alfred de Souza, 1980, *Women in Contemporary India and South Asia*. New Delhi: Manohar Publications.

Altekar, A.S., 1962, *The Position of Women in Hindu Civilization*. Delhi: Motilal Banarasidass.

——, 1991, *The Position of Women in Hindu Civilization*. Delhi: Motilal Banarasidass Publishers.

Amadiume, I, 1989, *Male Daughters, Female Husband, Gender and Sex in the African Society*. London: Zed Book Ltd.

Andal, N., 2002, *Women and Indian Society—Options and Constraints*, Jaipur: Rawat Publications.

Arputhamurthy, S., 1990, *Women at Work and Discrimination*, New Delhi: Ashish.

Arya, Anita, 2000, *Indian Women*, New Delhi: Gyan Publishing House.

Atray, J.P., 1988, *Crimes Against Women*. New Delhi: Vikas Publishing House.

Austin, H.S., and Bayer, A.E., 1973, "Sex Discrimination in Academic", In Alice S. Rosai and A. Calderwood, eds. *Academic Women on the Move*. New York: Russel Sage.

Bagehi Jasodhara, 1995, *Indian Women—Myth and Reality*, ed. Calcutta: Sangam Books.

Bagwe, Anjali, 1995, *Of Women Caste—The Experience of Gender in Rural India*. Calcutta: STREE.

Bakken Tin, 2000, "Constitutional and Social Equality: Legacies and Limits at Law, Politics and Culture", *Indian, Journal of Gender Studies*, Vol. 7(1): 71-82.

Baligar, V.P.V., 1999, *Mother and Girl Child—Reconstructing Attitudes*. Jaipur: Rawal Publications.

BMC, 1997, *Population Profile of Slums in Bhubaneswar., (Unpublished)*.

Baral, J.A., and Patnaik, K., 1990, *Gender Politics*. Columbia: Discovery Publishing House.

Barry H, M. Bacon and I. Child, 1957, "A Cross-Cultural Survey of Some Sex Differences in Socialisation", *Journal of Abnormal and Social Psychology*. 55:327-32.

Basu, Monmayee, 2001, *Hindu Women and Marriage Law—From Sacrament to Contract*. New Delhi: Oxford University Press.

Berrett, M., 1980, *Women's Oppression Today*. London: Verso.

Bhadra, Mita, 1992, *Women Workers of Tea Plantation in India*, New Delhi: Heritage.

Buler, G., 1964, *The Law of Manu*, trans in Muller, M.ed, Sacred Books of the East, XXV, Delhi: Motilal Banarasidass.

Chatterji Shoma, A, 2000, *Indian Women—From Darkness to Light*. Calcutta: Parumita Publishers.

Chattopadhay, K., 1983, *Indian Women's Battle for Freedom*. New Delhi: Abhinav Publications.

Chandra Jaishree, 1993, "*Women and Child*". Jaipur: Rawat Publishers.

Chen, L.C. et al, 1981, "Sex Bias in the Family Allocation of Food and Health Care in Rural Bangladesh," *Population and Development Review,* 7(1): 55-70.

Chodorow, N, 1971, "Family Structure and Feminine Personality", in Richardson and Taylor, eds. *Feminist Frontiers II Relating Sex, Gender and Society*. New York: McGraw Hill.

Chung, B. et al, 1972, *Psychological Perspectives: Family Planning in Korea*. Seoul: Holly M.

Cormark, M, 1961, *The Hindu Women,* Bombay: Asia Publishing House.

Davis, K. and Balke, J. 1956, "Social Structure and Fertility: An Analytical Framework", *Economic Development and Cultural Change*. IV: 211-35.

Dayaram Gidumal, 1989, *The Status of Women in India*. New Delhi: Publications India.

Devendra Kiran, 1994, *Changing Status of Women in India,* New Delhi: Vikas Publishing House Pvt. Ltd.

Devi, G., 1967, "A Study of Sex Difference in Reaction to Frustration Situation", *Psychological Studies,* 12: 17-27.

Devi K. Uma, 2000, *Women's Equality in India*. New Delhi: Discovery Publishing House.

Devi, Lalitha U, 1982, *Status and Employment of Women in India*. Delhi: B.R. Publishing House.

Dixon, R., 1976, "Measuring Equality Between the Sexes", *Journal of Social Issues,* 32: 19-13.

Dworkin, S., 1991, "Can We Save the Girl?" *New Direction for Women,* Sept./Oct.: 3-4.

Espiritu Y.L., 1997, *Asian and American Women and Men*. Thousand Oaks: Sage Publications.

Everett Jana Matson, 1981, *Women and Social Change in India*. New Delhi: Heritage.

Feinman, S., 1981 "Why is Cross-Sex Role Behaviour More Approved for Girls than for Boys? A Status Characteristic Approach," *Sex Roles* 7:289-300.

Forum Against Rape, 1980, "Sex Role Expectations on Children's Vocational Aspirations and Perceptions of Occupations", *Psychology of Women Quarterly*. 8: 59-68.

Fracois Ey Rand, 1933, "Equal Pay and Value of Work in Industrialised Countries", *International Labour Review*, Vol. 132.

Ghadially, Rehana, 1988, *Women in Indian Society*. ed. New Delhi: Sage.

Ghosh, S., 1987, "The Female Child in India—A Struggle for Survival, "*NFI Bulletin* 8 (4).

Ghose, V, 1994, *Women in Society*. Singapore: Times Books International.

Gill, Kulwart, 1986, *Hindu Women's Right to Property in India*. New Delhi: Deep and Deep Publications.

Gol, 1989, *Development of Women and Child Development, The Lesser Child, The Girl in India*. New Delhi.

——, 1991, *Village Census Abstract, Bhubaneswar Block* (Unpublished).

——, 1998, *Women and Men in India*, New Delhi: Central Statistical Organisation.

Gopalan C., and Kaur S., 1989, *Women and Nutrition in India*. New Delhi: Nutrition Foundation of India.

Gothoskar, S., 1992, *Struggles of Women at Work*. New Dehi: Vikas.

Goulds, Sharon, 1986, *The Role of Women*. London: Macdonald & Co. (Publishers) Ltd.

Gupta, G.R., 1976, *Family and Social Change in India*. New Delhi: Vikas Publication House.

Gupta, S.N., 1978, *The Indian Concept of Values*. New Delhi: Manohar Book Service.

Gupta, Sumit & Mittal, Mukta, 1995, *Status of Women and Children in India*. eds. New Delhi: Anmol Publications Pvt. Ltd.

Hanumappa, H.G. & Sujatha, T.M., 1992, "The Changing Status of Rural Women", *Women and Development*. ed. Kalbagh, C, New Delhi: Discovery Publishing House.

Harriss-While Barbara, 2001, "A Note on Male Government of South Indian Family Business and its Implications for Women", *Indian Journal of Gender Studies*. 8 (1): 89-98.

Hasan, N., 1972, *The Social Security System in India*. New Delhi: S. Chand and Co. Pvt. Ltd.

Hawley, John S., 1994, *Sati, the Blessing and the Course: The Burning of Wives in India*. New York: Oxford University Press.

Heer, David M., 1958, "Dominance of Working Wife", *Social Forces*, 35: 341-47.

Holter, H., 1970, *Sex Roles and Social Structure*, Oslo: Universities for Larger.

Hoyenga, K.B. and K.T. Hoyenga, 1979, *The Question of Sex Difference: Psychological, Cultural and Biological Issues*. Boston: Little Brown.

Hussain Sabiha, 2003, "Gender and Reproductive Behaviour: The Role of Men", *Indian Journal of Gender Studies* 10 (1): 45-76.

Indra, 1955, *The Status of Women in Ancient India*, Banaras: Oriental Publishers and Booksellers.

Jain, D., 1975, *Indian Women*. New Delhi: Govt. of India.

Jain Jasbir and Supriya Agarwal, 2002, *Gender and Narrative*. Jaipur: New Delhi.

Jaiswal, R.P., 1993, *Professional Status of Women*. Jaipur: Rawat Publications.

Jha U.M., A. Mehta & L. Menon, 1998, *Status of Indian Women-Crisis and Conflict in Gender Issues*. Vol. 1, eds., New Delhi: Kanishka Publishers and Distributor.

Jha U.S. & P. Jani, 1996, *Indian Women Today—Tradition, Modernity and Challenge*, Vol. 1, eds. New Delhi: Kanishka Publishers and Distributors.

Jones, C.A., 1980, "Observations on the Current Status of Women in India", *International Journal of Women's Studies*. 3: 1-18.

Jones, R., 1973, "Sex Predetermination and the Sex Ratio at Birth", *Social Biology*, 20: 303-308.

Karlekar, M., 1987, *Poverty and Women's Work*. New Delhi: Shakti Books.

Kasturi, Malavika, 2000, "Female Infanticide: Selection from the Records of the Govt. of the North Western Provinces, Second Series, Vol. VIII, Allahabad, 1871" *Indian Journal of Gender Studies,* Vol. 7 (1): 125-134.

Kaushik, Vijay, 1997, *Women's Movement and Human Rights*. Jaipur: Pointer Publishers.

Kelly, J.A. and Coorell, L., 1976, "Parent Behaviours Related to Masculine, Feminine and Androgynous Sex Role Orientations", *Journal of Consulting and Clinical Psychology,* 44: 843-51.

Khanna, S.K., 2001, Jat and Pahari Jatni: Gendered Ethnicity in an Urbanising Village in North India. *The Anthropologist*. 3 (1): 11-19.

Khan, M.A. and Ayesha N., 1982, *Status of Rural Women in India*. New Delhi: Uppal Publishing House.

Kimmel, M.S., 2000, *The Gendered Society,* New York: Oxford University Press.

Kodoth, Praveena, 2001, "Gender, Family and Property Rights: Questions from Kerala's L and Reforms" *Indian Journal of Gender Studies*. 8 (2): 291-306.

Komarovsky, Mirra, 1950, "Functional Analysis of Sex Roes". *American Sociological Review*. 15: 508-16.

——, 1973, "Cultural Contradiction and Sex Roles: The Masculine Case", *American Journal of Sociology*. 78: 873-85.

Kumar Ashok, 1989, *Indian Women Towards 21st Century*. New Delhi: Criterion.

Kumari Ranjana, 1988, *Brides are not for Burning: Dowry Victims in India:* New York: Radiant Publishers.

Lakshmi Kumari, M., 1997, *The Role of Women in Society—Sita Must Live*. New Delhi: Sterling Publishers Pvt. Ltd.

Madan, T.N., 1975, "The Hindu Women at Home", in D. Jain ed., *Indian Women,* New Delhi: Govt. of India.

Madden, J.F., 1981, "Why Women Work Close to Home", *Urban Studies*. 18: 181-94.

Mead Margaret, 1935, *Women, Position in Society Encyclopedia of Social Science*, Vol. XV. New York: The Mc Millan Company.

Megargee, E.I., 1969, "Influence of Sex-Roles on the Manifestation of Leadership", *Journal of Applied Psychology*. 53: 377-82.

Mengista, D., 1994, "The Right of the Child", in Saksena K.P. ed. *Human Rights: Perspective and Challenges*. New Delhi: Lancers Books.

Mittal, M., 1995, *Women Power in India*, ed. New Delhi: Anmol Publications Pvt. Ltd.

Mitter, Sara S., 1992, *Dharma's Daughters: Contemporary Indian Women and Hindu Culture*. New Brunswick: Rutgers University Press.

Montagu, A., 1968, *The Thermal Superiority of Women*. New York: Mac Millan.

Mukherjee, Prabhati, 1978, *Hindu Women—Normative Models*. Calcutta: Orient Longman.

Mutharayappa, R., – "Is Culture Influencing Family Planning Acceptance", *Man in India*, 81 (3-4): 277-289.

Mukherjee, Rona, 1997, *Legal Status and Remedies for Women in India*. New Delhi: Deep and Deep Publications.

Nagaich Sangeeta, 1997, *Changing Status of Women in India*, New Delhi: Anmol Publications Pvt. Ltd.

Nandy, A., 1975, "Sati, or a Nineteenth Century Tale of Women, Violence, and Protest in V.C. Joshi ed., *Rammohan Roy and the Problem of Modernization in India*, New Delhi: Vikas.

Nair, P.T., 1978, *Marriage and Dowry in India*. Colombia: South Asia Books.

Nirmala Bhai, P., 1981, *Harijan Women in Independent India*. New Delhi: B.R. Publishing Corporation.

Ortner, S.B., 1974, "Is Female to Male as Nature is to Culture?" in M.Z. Rosaldo and L. Lamphere eds. *Woman, Culture and Society*, Stanford University Press.

Pant, Niranjan, 1995, *Status of Girl Child and Women in India,* New Delhi: APH.

Phadke, S., 1976, "Special Problems of Education of Women", in M.S. Gore, I.P. Desai and Sama Chitnis. eds. *Papers in the Sociology of Education in India*. New Delhi: NCERT.

Phillips, W.S.K., 1994, *Street Children in India,* Jaipur: Rawat Publications.

Pohlman, E.H., 1969, *The Psychology of Birth Planning Shenkuan.* Cambridge: MASS.

Poplin, D.E. (ed), 1978, *Social Problems.* London: Foresman & Co.

Prabhu, P., 1962, *Hindu Social Organisation.* Bombay: Popular Book Depot.

Priya, 1992, "Struggle for Equal Rights for Women Contract Workers of Ennore Thermal Power Station" in S. Gothaskar (ed) *Women at Work.* New Delhi: Vikas.

Puri, Nina, 1998, "The Girl Child in India", in the *Journal of Family Welfare,* Vol. 44.

Purusothaman, S., 1998, The Empowerment of Women in India, New Delhi: Sage.

Ram Chandra Bindu, 2001, 'Gaddika'—Male Ritual in a Patrilineal Society as a Cultural Paradign, *The Anthropologist* 3 (1): 29-31.

Rao, K.V. and D. Krishna, N. Balakrishna 2000, "Gender Differentials in Malnutrition—A Case Study of Pre-school Children", *Man in India,* 80 (3-4): 289-294.

Rosaldo, M.Z. and Lamphere L., 1974, *Women, Culture and Society: A Theoretical Overview.* California: Stanford University Press.

Sachhidananda and R.P. Sinha, 1984, *Women's Rights: Myth and Reality.* Jaipur: Printwell Publishers.

Sastri Madhu, 1990, *Status of Hindu Women,* Jaipur: RBSA Publishers.

Scarlett T. Epstein and Rohmaey A. Walts, 1981, *The Endless Day.* ed. Oxford: Pergamon Press.

Sen, Indrani, 2001, "Devoted Wife/Sensuous Bibi: Colonial Constructions of the Indian Women, 1860-1900" *Indian Journal of Gender Studies*, 8 (1): 1-22.

Sharma, B.R., 1997, *Women, Marriage, Family, Violence and Divorce*, Jaipur: Mangal Deep Publications.

Sharma, B.R. and Pruthi, Raj, 1995, *International Dimension of Women's Problems*. New Delhi: Anmol Publications Pvt. Ltd.

Sharma, Vijay, 1994, *Problems to Women in Matrimonial Home*. New Delhi: Deep and Deep Publications.

Smoker, B, 1975, "Women and the Patriarchal God", *The Secularist*. 33: 67-68.

Sohani, N.K., 1990, *Child Without Childhood*, Report on Girl Child Submitted to UNICEF, Mimeo New York: UNICEF (A Summary based on this report was published and issued by UNICEF in 1990).

——, 1994, *Status of Girl in Development Strategies*. New Delhi: Har-Anand Publications.

Sood, Rita, 1991, *Changing Status and Adjustment of Women*. New Delhi: Manak.

Souza, S.D and L. Chen, 1979, *Sex Biases of Mortality Differentials in Rural Bangladesh*, Bangladesh: International Centre for Diarrhoeal Research.

Stephen, Cole, 1986, "Sex Discrimination and Admission to Medical School—1929-1984". *American Journal of Sociology*. 92: 549-67.

Subramanyam, K., 1991, *Women and Law*. Hyderabad: Asia Law House.

Tandon, R.K., 1998, *Status of Women in Contemporary World*. New Delhi: Commonwealth Publishers.

Tellis-Nayak, J.B and M.L. Brito, 1992, *Indian Women Forge Ahead*. New Delhi: Indian Social Institute.

The Dharitree, 1999, "Nari", 29.9.99.

The Samaj, 1998, "Bharatiyamananka Harahari Paramayu Athasathi Varsa-Budhabudhi Manaka Varanaposana Pain Jatiyastratre Aaina Heba", in The Samaj, (in Oriya), 6.4.1998. Cuttack: Lokasevak Mandal.

——, 1999, "Patibrayta Phala" 8.6.1999, Cuttack.

——, 1999, "Jhia Janam Hebaru Nirjyatana", 24.7.1999, Cuttack.

——, 1999, "Mai Masaru Sarbanimna Majuri 60 Tanka", Cuttack.

The *Telegraph*, 1999, "Daughter of Joy", 1.8.99.

The *Times of India*, 1999, "Women Tonsured for Adultery", 28.7.99.

Willamson, N., 1976, *Sons or Daughters: A Cross-Cultural Survey of Parental Preferences*. Beverly Hills: Sage.

UNICEF, 1990, *The Girl Child An Investigation in the Future*, New York.

——, 1994, *The Right to be a Child*", UNICEF India Background Paper, March, New Delhi.

Upadyay, H.C., *Status of Women in India*, Delhi: Anmol Publications.

Verma, G.R., B.V. Babu and A. Rohni, 2000, "A Study on Knowledge of Various Family Planning Methods among Rural Populations of Andhra Pradesh", *Man in India*, 80 (3-4): 331-336.

Victor R. Fuchs, 1988, *Women's Quest for Economic Equality*. London: Harvard University Press.

Vijayan, A, 1992, *Fish Workers Collective Struggle for Change the Role of Women*, New Delhi: Vikas.

Index